Step Up and SHINE: Power and Presence in Action

Five Keys to Unlock Your Soul-Inspired Business, Using Practical and Spiritual Practices

Dedication:

I would like to thank my family, my husband, and countless other people for helping me bring my idea for this book to life. My coaches—Therese Skelly, Erin Owen, Sharon Wilson, and Brooke Lieb—were all important to me. My spiritual mentors—Ron Young, Rick Jarow, and Vivien Schapera—gave me the anchor into the spiritual world that has influenced my outlook and ability to help others heal.

My clients—Carla Zackson Heller, Barbara Pichon, Noreen Haren, Ed Smith, Angela Suter, Lynn Mullins, Mara Bragg, Nancy Kranich, Claire Berkowitz, Nicky Isaacson,

Lily Hareem, Barbara Strogatz, Aletia Morgan, and many others—have given me the extraordinary opportunity to share my wisdom; their insights and their willingness to learn from me help to form the great circle of trust that goes far to move consciousness and healing forward.

Every one of my friends and family members have given to me from their hearts, and that gift has helped me to cultivate optimism and the faith that my voice matters. A particular thank you to Lawrence Feinberg and Neil M. Sussman, who support me in countless ways. I would be so much less without them.

Preface

If you have been feeling frustrated because you know you have a greater purpose in life but are stuck in patterns and ways of being that keep you limited and small—and you are ready to finally get moving with the dreams you have put on the back burner—this book is for you. If you are a healer, a helping professional, or a highly sensitive entrepreneur and have been wondering how to connect more deeply with your own intuition to show you the way to direct your business focus, you are in the right place. My intention for writing this book is to help you get your spark ignited and to engage your full prosperity consciousness, to stop waiting or second-guessing yourself, and to stop hiding out in your life.

It is time for you to make your freedom-based business and lifestyle headline news so that your ideal clients can find you, so that you can ask for business with all of the clarity and security that your heart knows is going to serve others, and so you will no longer be the best-kept secret in your field. Would you like to end the struggle and get on the easy road to true business bliss? This book creates a powerful container for you to take up the mantle and work on your own transformation: to connect deeply with your soul-inspired visions and then fill in the details of actually living your dreams from the blueprint of your most cherished vision.

Contrary to popular opinion, going for your dreams doesn't have to be hard or drag you through the underworld. You can make the decision to take the fast track to living on your terms, creating a business you love. and living a soul-inspired life. The only thing you have to do is to say "Yes, I want this!" and start to let things unfold. Don't worry about the how for now.

Sound a little too easy? Let me just say that if you don't figure this out now you will be dragging your feet for a long time and, most likely, will not see much change. Do you want to really be on purpose and shine in your life? Here is a blueprint for you.

You must be willing to create the space and time to clearly envision what you want to manifest in your business so that you can harness your marketing brilliance and bring your insightful wisdom to work for you. The results will help you problem-solve easily, help you to find the right solutions for any confusion that comes up as well as thinking and acting like the strong leader you are.

You begin with a deep listening to the body, of caring for yourself. You gather the resolve to really believe in yourself on all levels—physically, emotionally, and spiritually—and be sure that you don't leave any aspect of yourself behind. You get to know your intuitive capacity as a decision maker for everything in your business. You guide all of your choices with calm conviction.

As you look inward and assess where you are at present, while allowing some patience for your process, you prioritize what is really important to you, and your energy does not get depleted or tangled. You anchor daily practices that matter to your wellbeing as you fill in the picture of the vision you are carrying.

You start doing something with the insights you have. It is no longer theoretical or "what if"; instead, you have a tangible plan to make your vision a reality, bringing you the money you want and the lifestyle you desire. You contribute your gifts and talents in a way that serves both you and the world, enjoying more impact as you continually elevate yourself and take on more challenges.

Your business reflects the confidence and influence you are developing in the doing of it, where you feel ready to speak intimately and truthfully about who you are and the service you provide in a way that builds trust, community, and wealth in the grandest sense of the word!

Diane Young Sussman
Philadelphia, 2020

You can find out more about Diane L. Sussman by going to her Website: http://www.healingintoabundance.com , where you can also get her FREE audio, "Vision, Value, and Visibility: 5 Keys to Having More Impact as a Spiritual Entrepreneur." Learn the secrets for holding your vision dear, upgrading your self-worth, and getting into action in your business, which will bring you increased sales and success. Imagine easily creating a luxury brand and celebrity status while contributing your talents.

Using both inner energy practices and outer practical strategies to align your business with your capacities, you can catapult the success of your business.

Testimonials:

"The guidance I received from Diane comes from such an authentic, natural place. She is powerfully intuitive and uses her gifts with a gentle, positive energy. Diane's unique way of sharing her wisdom is exceptional, and she has led me with grace and loving compassion every step of the way. I have tapped into a deep place of *knowing* that I am on my path to realizing my dreams, and I am forever grateful."
Debra Fisher, MBA, Carlsbad, California

"I have been talking up a storm about Diane's "Heart of Money" course to friends: the best testimonial I can offer! Diane has been a fantastic coach; timely with her comments; exquisitely attuned to my needs, my personality type, and right on target with it all. If you want to focus on money to change your life, please consider taking her course; it will change your relationship to both.
Ute Arnold, MFA, Mt Pleasant, Pennsylvania
Body-Psychotherapist, Artist, Author. www.unergi.com

Copyright © 2020 Diane L. Sussman. All rights reserved. No portion of this book may be reproduced mechanically, electronically, or by any other means—including photocopying—without written permission of the publisher. It is illegal to copy this book, post it to a Website, or distribute it by any other means without permission from the publisher.

Diane L. Sussman

2018 Green St, Philadelphia, PA 19130

(646) 734-7179

Diane@healingintoabundance.com

www.healingintoabundance.com

Limits of Liability and Disclaimer of Warranty

The author and publisher shall not be liable for your misuse of this material. This book is strictly for informational and educational purposes.

Warning – Disclaimer

The purpose of this book is to educate and entertain. The author and/or publisher do not guarantee that anyone following these techniques, suggestions, tips, ideas, or strategies will become successful. The author and/or publisher shall have neither liability nor responsibility to anyone with respect to any loss or damage caused, or alleged to be caused, directly or indirectly, by the information contained in this book.

This book provides a mindset-boosting taste of what it would look like to fully reveal your gifts and talents both to yourself and in the world, to confidently speak from whatever stage you choose, to experience ease over struggle, thriving over striving, and gently settle into your natural flow as the CEO of your own business. Are You Ready to Step Up and SHINE?

Introduction:

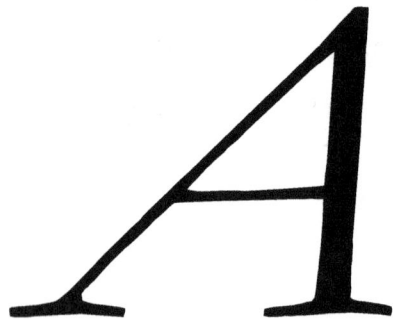

A soul-inspired life is a life that bends toward the whisperings of your inner longing.

Diane L. Sussman

The time is now. Are you ready for a mind-shifting experience in which you can touch the very essence of your talents and gifts and find a way to bring them fully into the world through your business? If you are not already living your dream by having daily contact with your ideal clients, sharing your inspired message, and transforming lives, you might need to turn up the volume of your visibility and take some new and bolder actions.

You have to ask yourself whether you are willing and able to take the steps necessary to unfold a business plan that is a perfect fit for who you are. Are you willing to do be the CEO of your own enterprise and the spiritual leader who manages the whole package for the vision you want to bring into the world?

If you have been feeling frustrated because you haven't felt fully seen or appreciated or had the proper attention paid to you for all of the efforts you have made to increase business exposure, it is time to think bigger.

But what if you never felt you had permission to speak your mind or live fully expressed and so have stayed hidden and quiet? What if you have, until now, only experienced your blocks to abundance and couldn't clear them? Wouldn't you be living at a lower level of your potential?

How would it make you feel to see others moving forward with their visions and dreams, but you felt you didn't have access to yours? And how much money would you be leaving on the table to not be involved fully in your life's passionate work, the work you were meant to do? If that door were closed to you, would you not feel the loss deeply?

I am here to offer you a little mindset-boosting experience that you can take to revisualize your healing practice or entrepreneurial business. I wish you the best possible outcome for your future. Together we will shine the light on what is not working in your business and find new ways to gain clarity on what you want to accomplish so that you can fully realize your heart-based work, and you can feel the satisfaction of living your life fully and with purpose.

Life is always providing opportunities to face limitations and blocks and to clear them so that you can move swiftly toward the divine path to which you are entitled. The end result is a huge movement toward your goals and dreams and a life well lived. You, and only you, can offer the precise recipe of service that your ideal clients desperately need so that they are able to step up to the life they too are meant to live. Therefore, it is not only for you, but also in service to your clients, that we are seeking clarity about your life's work.

If you couldn't or didn't want to step up to your capabilities, some part of your spirit would remain unexpressed.

And, even more importantly, those whom you were meant to serve through your good work would not find you and would therefore not be served.

You are a spiritual leader, a way-shower and guide for others, but if you keep your light hidden and your gifts buried in the sand, nobody will benefit from your teachings. You are here for a reason. As you decide to participate fully in the marketplace, you play in the field of your potential. It is your divine destiny that you will see unfold before you with the precise amount of juice you put into it. Decades could easily pass before you wake up and listen to your inner calling and step forward into your divine path, taking on all that you are meant to do. So why not start now?

We live in community with one another to bring forward the best that life allows. The world is waiting; abundance and growth are available to you at all times. To not believe that you are a part of the greater good of life is to be blocked from your inheritance, and that requires healing. As you heal you can release your unnamed fears and doubts and draw on the support that will awaken you to what is best for you and your potential clients.

So are you living "full throttle" toward your dreams, or do you feel somewhat blocked? Most likely, if you feel blocked, you are bumping up against some attitudes of your personal history where the frayed edges and sharp corners of life have damaged you. Well, again I say the time is now to make some commitments to change!

My greatest joy is to participate with other conscious entrepreneurs in the magnificent unfolding of our world's evolution. I help those who want to get closer to the full expression of their soul's divine purpose and live from that rich place to bring their leadership out more fully, easily, and abundantly. No fear, no worry, no confusion or sense of being overwhelmed need be present because all of those lower-level energies will be cleared and no longer competing for mind time.

You can move swiftly toward your dreams and goals and create simple systems to follow that will make your life easier and your business flourish.

The one thing we have available to do the perfect next thing for our businesses is simply to listen to what needs to be expressed. Business happens one step at a time.

Knowing, and taking action on the right next step, makes all the difference for the outcome.

You are building your dream business from a place of deep inner knowledge and trust. You are doing your marketing from a place of clarity and faith. You are looking outside yourself for opportunities that may not even feel like opportunities in the moment, but you are guided by your listening and your intuition.

And here is a secret. You don't have to have everything in place before you get out there and start to speak about what it is that you do. In fact, you must start speaking before you think you are ready, because only then do people and circumstances come into view when opportunities are revealed to you as exciting next steps. Your success is measured not by having all of the pieces in place beforehand but by acting on trust and faith that you will be given help because you have the vision.

In a sense, you are connecting with other people through your inner guidance. Think of it as an aligned knowing. Your inner guidance reveals what is at your fingertips! Have courage; there really is no better way or better path than following your intuition to get what you want in life.

Yes, you must clear the resistance, as it inevitably comes up, and listen quietly for which doors to start opening. Ultimately, we are here to support and assist each other in our spiritual development, and the best way possible to that end is to create from your own voice first, which inspires you and allows you to connect with what is most meaningful for you.

It is my intention to help you activate a deep desire to go after your imaginative vision so that you can take on the activation of your own soul's gifts.

All of your experiences matter because this is the way you learn and change. You are guided both by the mistakes you have made, the obstacles along your journey, and all the magic that has shown up for you along the way. There are many synchronicities in life that lead you in the right direction. If you have to go down a difficult path for a while for your soul to grow and mature, then that is what is up for you. If you take the easy path through a deep faith in the Universe to have your back, all the better.

I believe we all have the potential to live from a connected center of belonging, one that creates unity instead of separation, where we can strive to serve with more determi nation and depth and participate in a healed vision of the world. How we tap into those resources and continually evolve brings sweetness to our lives as well as more clarity and understanding about how life serves us and how we serve life through helping each other to thrive.

There is no need for competition, judgment, or suspicion of others. We can grow even through the bad things that happen, which may be just as important in our evolution. We have the option to take on as much responsibility for spiritual growth as we choose.

So my question to you is: Are you living a soul-inspired life? Do you know who you truly are, what you have come here to complete or to begin? Have you asked for help through whatever form it may come: books, dreams, meditation, spiritual teachers? And do you have the courage and the drive to go further, deeper?

If you are frightened to go through what you perceive as uncomfortable experiences, feel the fear and do it anyway so that you can break through the tough first layer of procrastination and fear and then be prepared to be surprised and delighted. See yourself going for a ride into the places and circumstances that open the curtain and reveal your fortune because they are the next best steps in the unfolding of your life journey. This is where you get to be the driver and the creator and where full expression is the gift.

You need a strong conviction and a clear sign post or two along the way. There will be challenges, of that there is no doubt, and part of your mind may be very determined to keep you safe and will do its best to keep you in the familiar and protected regions of your present-day existence. Your ego is not very interested in intrigue, mystery, or danger, so the choice to act upon your gut feelings about what comes next will have to be much stronger than the quick-fix choices that keep you protected. Those quick-fix choices will keep you invisible and prevent you from being seen, heard, known, and remembered.

This vision often feels hidden and obscured to you, but if you could really touch and awaken it, this could be the true voice of your divine nature calling you forward.

Imagine having the insight and inner resources to be listening to your eternal self, not the ego self that is always fearful and never challenging you. Imagine quieting the small voice inside that tries to keep you small and protected; instead, feel yourself listening to the voice of your heart that says, "Yes, this is what I want! This is the way! Go here!" even if it might seem scary or dangerous or wrong.

What could happen if you were to take action on the opportunities that are right in front of you? It might cost you an investment in time, money: indeed, sometimes more money than you ever imagined spending. But it could lead you closer to your goal. And the reward would come back to you one hundredfold.

So, if the opportunity eludes you or, worse still, doesn't present itself as an opportunity at all, what happens? You stay just where you are with all of your ideas and imagination faltering because you don't have a means of expression. Dreams dashed, the picture fading.

It is said that when you say yes to your dreams and desires, really say yes to them, the Universe will conspire to bring you exactly what you have asked for because you have made the decision to say yes. If you waver on that decision, the energy of the activation dissipates, effectively saying you actually don't want what you are saying you want. It is saying no to the possibility. Then the desired object acts like a wavering target that cannot be found and therefore cannot present the appropriate resources to you to fulfill your intention.

The very first thing you must do is to connect with what you most desire and choose it, no matter what. It is not for you to know how things are going to unfold, only that you place your attention and your intention where they can take root.

You soul is whispering to you to grow. You will inevitably be faced with all of your resistance anyway so just allow yourself to expect road-blocks. The creative mind looks at these blocks as creative problems to solve. Do you need more support? Do you need a personal assistant or a technical wizard to help you? Do you need more structure, a container to bring the idea to fruition? Do you need a business coach or personal empowerment coach to help you keep your mindset in a high state of vibration? Then get one.

Don't listen to that other voice that tells you that you cannot afford the things you need right now. Hire these people. When you do you are saying out loud that you are serious about your dream, you are a professional. You are also saying to the Universe that you know you can't be a one-woman show and try to do it all yourself, that you live in community of like-minded people who bring each other forward. You will find the people to help you if you ask. You will find the money to pay for them because their job is to help you bring your vision forward.

The cost of not doing this is much greater than the reward for making the decision to receive help. It is not about "I can't afford it." If you go to the rational part of your thinking mind too often, you choke off the parts of your vision that require assistance to flow properly. The way money comes into your business may be through a process that is not clear to you at the time, but will reveal itself as you accept and receive the mystery of "How" it comes.

You give of yourself, your gifts, and your light, and the money eventually comes back to you in the form of clients and revenue. You go out and ask for the business, and money is the return. You get yourself seen, and the people who are meant to work with you will be excited to be in your presence; they know that you are the one who can help them solve their problems. If you are too scared to put yourself in the limelight because you don't feel quite ready, they will not know you are available. It is that simple. You have no choice. You have to get over yourself! You have to start dancing in the flow.

What if you were a life coach and you really wanted more clients to work with but you didn't have your own coach because you didn't believe you had the money to spend on that level of support for your business?

Or what if you were a massage therapist or nutritionist who has not received a session of your own for so long you are forgetting your craft? When you step out in faith and do what you love everything starts to fall in line for you. However, if you hold back and don't give yourself the same caring treatment you are offering others, this too will be noticed on some level, and your alignment will be somewhat off.

The other downside of this approach is that you will inevitably attract people who themselves have issues with money or what I call a "lack" mentality. People who will expect a lot for a little, try to take advantage of your time and resources, or think they can receive your services free of charge.

The congruence in your energy is connected to your integrity. It is grounded in your trust and faith in the flow of life, which includes the flow of abundant resources that we all get to enjoy. As you understand this principle, you will have much more courage to trust that the invisible connections of nature and the Universe are connected to you.

This is an energy-management concept. So, if you are having trouble attracting the people you want to work with, you might first look into this area and see if you can change your attitude and trust that things will work out for you if you put yourself forward.

However, if you know your value and you are willing to invest highly in your learning and healing, you will attract high-level, high-paying clients who are happy to receive from you, refer you to their friends, and use the wisdom you give to create abundance in their lives.

Another way "lack" mentality shows up in your life is in living small. Because you have the attitude that you "don't have the money" to pay for what you need, you attempt to try to do everything yourself and get easily overwhelmed and confused. Then, the ability to show a clear and consistent brand and presence is obscured, and you won't have the success you envision for yourself.

You get easily discouraged, and you may start to lose faith in your work. You might feel like a failure and be on the edge of giving up. Your inner guidance will always lead you away from that kind of thinking, but you don't

listen. Your mind says you cannot pay for support but your guidance is whispering to take the leap of faith to get to the next level.

It is so close, yet you are afraid to jump and break through. So what voice are you listening to? Listening to your inner guidance has to do with generating a higher vibrational output. Let me explain. Everything in life holds an energetic vibration. Think of how a telephone rings or a cell phone vibrates when someone is calling. The vibration has an amplitude or frequency rate. When your heart beats quickly it has a high frequency of movement. Energy vibrates also. Light is a high vibration, sound a lower one. When you can adjust your energy frequency, you can hold more light, and this is a good thing.

Studies have shown that depression and shame hold low frequency; joy and ecstasy hold high frequency. You thoughts actually affect your biology. This is why healing modalities such as Energy Work and Reiki have proven success records. You can actually change your frequency by changing your thoughts, thereby bringing more freedom and ease into your life. The challenge is to keep listening for your inner guidance and clearing the dense and heavy energies as they inevitably come up in the form of reactive resistance and self-sabotage. You are teaching yourself to activate a higher level of energy that supports a new level of self- approval and enthusiasm.

There are blocks to abundance that take the form of guilt and shame, of feelings of loss, beliefs transferred from parents and guardians and within the culture itself that keep us from living and behaving in more expansive ways. My observation and experience is that life will constantly bring up negative emotions for us to clear. This is how the mind works; it gets locked into your history and keeps recreating and embellishing thoughts and stories to support loss. The soul's journey is all about giving you experiences in order to clear past attitudes and beliefs so you can evolve and experience a larger and fuller expression of life.

The goal, of course, is full mastery of all that you do. Why should other people become masterful and you remain a servant to your fears? If you continue a course of lack and scarcity and not believing in yourself, you will not have the momentum necessary to get out and share your gifts. Why not live to the fullest possible expression of your potential? As you meet your pain and suffering consciously and head-on, you have an opportunity to shift your consciousness to that full expression.

It feels like freedom, beauty, and pleasure. It looks like harmony, music, and dance. It is you in flow and in full playful expression, a manifestation of your bigger, wiser self. Its vibration is so full of light that you radiate. People see you as a beacon of positive energy and feminine presence, and they are drawn to you. You become magnetic! People are filled by your energy, and you are setting an example for them to become magnetic themselves.

As you step into your mastery, you begin to see many old ways of being to fall away. People who kept you down disappear from your life. Opportunities and synchronicities that never before came your way suddenly appear, and you see your influence grow. You are living in a higher vibratory field, and what you want is easily available to you because your attention is moving in a more defined and refined way.

You let go of your frustration, confusion, and that which overwhelms you and welcome more simplicity and ease into your life. You are, in fact, dancing with the natural forces of nature and the Universe to assist you in becoming what you want to be. You will release the old, worn out patterns that no longer serve you but were just what you inherited from family and society. Why not make a concerted effort to change all that? You will have so much more available to you. You will be listening to your own drummer, leaning toward the whisperings of your own soul.

Chapter One: Begin Where You Are

Have you ever blamed other people for your misfortunes?

Do you have stories inside that go something like this:

"The reason I cannot get ahead is because _____ doesn't let me. The reason I cannot do _____ is because _____ has never given me opportunities. I have _____illness so I cannot do what I really want to do. I don't have (money, time, energy) to invest in my dream business, so I will put it on the back burner for now. There is always next year..."

You get the picture. This is called the blame game. You are creating a story in your mind about the limitations that exist in your life, and you are choosing to let them keep you stuck.

Key Number 1 is to begin where you are. There is only one way out of this situation, which is to take 100% responsibility for every thought, feeling, behavior, and action in your life. Yes, 100% responsibility no matter what. This may be the hardest thing you have ever done because your habits are deeply ingrained in your psyche, as are each of your excuses.

The reason you are the way you are points to deeply held beliefs that must be cleared for you to move forward and be the leader that you are meant to be. You must learn to "read" your energy. The energy of excuses is a very low vibrational energy. It actually makes you more ill, not less. There is not enough life energy to draw on so you are stealing it from the resources you would otherwise use to heal and create.

Your energy field and your body get locked into attitudes and postures that are very difficult to unlock and you go down, down, down.

Most people I know who spend their life energy blaming others for their problems also have physical or mental malaise as well. They cannot acquire enough physical energy to overcome the inertia of the body, and they sink into a terrible state of lassitude. Sooner or later other physical problems get loaded onto the first ones, and the energy field becomes even more clogged and troubled. It is very difficult to climb out of this place without help.

But the key to turning around this situation is to begin right where you are. How do I know this for certain? This was my story. I had a well- embellished tale about an auto-immune illness that was the "reason" for my difficulties.

I talked about my disease, felt it live in me daily, and carried it around with me without ever putting it down even for a moment. I was aware that I may be a co-creator in my problem, but the story was very strong and I got a lot of fuel for it by the constant re-telling. I had, and still have a lupus-like rash on my face that embarrassed me, and I had constant fatigue, so the disease felt real to me. I fought to rid myself of it, but that was part of the problem. The healing came in the awareness that I needed more love in my life, not more fight. I was going about

the problem in the wrong way. In fact, my healing required that I actually shift my whole outlook about illness. This is the reason I am sharing with you. Had I been the picture of good health, I may have never inquired about spiritual healing at all. I would have lived my life without a burning need to understand and change my energetic output. And so my passion to
heal led to a lifetime study and passion for healing, which has revealed my life's purpose.

So, my wish for you is to be willing to begin right where you are now, breathe in the present like the true mystery that it is, and appreciate all the insights you have. Be present to yourself without agenda and without story for the moment and be willing not to have to talk about it.

Know that you are loved beyond measure, and that any and all your hardships can be released as if they never existed in the first place: cleansed like a spring rain softly kissing your cheeks and shoulders. Sit still and decide that you can begin again right now.

The key is for you to find a way to begin to slow down and listen with softness to your own breath, your own inner wealth that is fully alive even with any physical or emotional pain you carry. Then be willing to take full responsibility for having brought yourself and your life to this moment in time and space. What power in that! Your creation, your life!

Stop, and listen. Listen to all the pain, all the things you are telling yourself about how you got here; just sit with it quietly. It is OK, and you are OK. Yes you have regrets. Yes you have a few apologies to make for hurting another person or two along the way.

There is some internal forgiving that could be done, and as well some external forgiving too. Or if you, in this moment, really wished that someone else had the resources to ask you for forgiveness of something of which you have felt wronged, that would be nice too, but probably will not happen.

In this moment you can quiet everything down and just listen to your breath and heartbeat.

You may start to experience memories and feelings resurfacing. Excellent! These need to be cleared and released. Release is a gift. You shouldn't be carrying around negative energy; it needs to be forgiven and forgotten.

This can be very sensitive territory. As many of my clients have struggled with this idea of forgiveness, I help them to see that the other person is most likely not carrying the energy that you are feeling, so forgiving the other is about healing you.

That person most likely dumped a load of something onto you and walked away unscathed and now you are holding it. It serves you to let it go and not allow the memories to continue to fester inside.

Or you are perhaps not needing to forgive the person, as that is not the point, but you must still forgive the tangled energy of being involved with that experience, and you are starting to let it fall back to the past where it belongs.

As you begin to take responsibility for your part in being in the situation, you can let go of the experience and find a way to categorize it as something your soul needed in order to learn and grow. If nothing else, you have "been there, done that." You don't have to call in another entangled circumstance like that one.

I know many women who finally disentangle themselves from a relationship with a man that has not served them and then fall into another relationship just like the previous one. This is an unconscious tendency to stay in the same familiar kind of relationship and not to release and renew from a deeper place of awareness and experience.

So life brings another person forward for you to keep trying to clear the same problem. Why not go instead to a deep place within your heart and mind and really try to understand why you needed that experience so that you don't have to repeat it?

Finally, we get to a more solid ground where the vision of something better outweighs the need to repeat a negative and charged experience, and we have finally released the energy. Life brings many opportunities to heal and grow. Ultimately, the awareness that we are infinite beings of great light dawns upon us, and we start creating from a much bigger and more beautiful center. This new attitude then draws healthier expressions of the possible and leads us beyond the difficulties and toward greater desires where full flourishing can commence.

Doing things for the wrong reasons—for example, the need to be loved and appreciated—may short-circuit a bigger and more soul-connected ability to listen and wait for greater expression and ease in our lives. It is only through taking stock of the patterns that have held us prisoners of our own beliefs that we can begin to make clean strides toward a more positive future. The work of release of the old ways of being has to come first, then the new-found freedom will bring its own rewards.

Now let's do a healing meditation

I would like you to come fully present to this moment and close your eyes. Take a few deep cleansing breaths and settle into yourself more deeply. Let your shoulders relax and your head nod a little forward. Relax behind your eyes, tongue, jaw. Take some time now to let go of all the stress and worry of the day, and just be. Sink your energy down into your hips, then down into the Earth where you can draw on the deep resources of the magnetic Divine energy of the Earth: nurturing, grounded, supportive.

Let that energy come to you, back through your feet and legs, your belly, and up into your heart. At the same time, let a beautiful light source come down from the heavens into your crown chakra, down to your forehead, clearing your third eye, your ears, your throat, your shoulders and arms, and into your heart. Let those two light sources meet in your heart area and let this light expand within you and around you. Let the light really expand now into the room and even 30 to 50 feet away from you. Let yourself bathe in light. This is the place where you will start to release your blocks to abundance and create new possibilities for your life.

You are sitting with yourself and welcoming in the co-creator energy that works through God/Spirit/Source. It is generative and creative, offering insight into new possibilities for your life and business. Take a few moments now to listen to what is speaking to you and ask yourself if there is anything negative in your life about which you have culpability. Is there anyone in your life in whom you have placed the power of control?

How old were you when you first gave your power away in this way? Are you willing to bring light to this block and clear it now? Whatever time, dimension, space, or reality this existed in, can you clear it now?

Now let a new vision of possibility come that can hold you in this space of deep loving energy. Let it fill you with its light and bring you into wholeness. Now give thanks, and, when you are ready, open your eyes.

We have just completed a clearing. Healing is all about releasing and clearing and then holding firm in your conviction not to be taken again into the energies of disempowerment. You are creating a new muscle of sorts, one that allows you to hold a higher vibration for yourself.

As you do this process over and over again, you will begin to see a lot of old patterns, behaviors, and beliefs start to release from your field. You will be attracting a new energy of possibility and light for your life and business. You are on your way to sensing and feeling a new kind of support and a vision or sense about the people who will assist you in the creation of your new dreams and desires. You come into more control of your destiny and champion a stronger foundation for the full flourishing of your life.

When I was in my twenties I heard women often talk about "coping" with their circumstances. Although I loved that word, I never used it in my daily speech and did not feel that I was in need of coping with my life. I was very lucky to be a dancer in New York City and spent my days in creative pursuits and evenings in an exciting, albeit exhausting restaurant in Greenwich Village: struggling maybe, but not coping!

I was more free than many because I was married without children and focusing on the creation of my dances and being the artistic co-director of a dance collective company: "Theater of the Heart." I was actually living the dream that I had come to New York to accomplish, and everything was going smoothly minus the incredible energy expenditure required to keep all the balls up in the air.

But women were talking about this "coping" idea, and I remember thinking what is it that I am missing here? I slowly realized that coping had to do with not living your own life. The people who were coping were actually complaining of being powerless in their lives, and they were unhappy about it. From my perspective, things looked fine for them; they tended to have a lot of material assets I didn't have.

But what they didn't have was personal power. These were young mothers who had very little control over their own lives and didn't seem to have any personal outlets for their creativity. I can say that I don't see so much of that these days; however, women are often still in situations in which they don't have leadership avenues, control, or decision-making power.

But the times have changed so much that anyone still in that position must take a second look at their belief systems and decide that she might not have to go down the path of the powerless woman but instead adopt a new paradigm. We are now witnessing an opening in consciousness in a big way. Our potential to make great things happen in the world is greater than in any previous era.

We have a huge opportunity to make a global impact, tithe to third-world countries so that they too can take advantage of the new world economy and be part of a world emerging as truly cooperative. As quickly as our consciousness can shift to manage the possibilities, we can change the way we do business. The new paradigm involves the collective values of shared visions instead of the each-one-out-for-himself outdated paradigm that was established in the past.

As we enter the workplace as leaders, we bring with us the ability for cooperation and shared vision. From early agrarian times, women have stayed at the hearth to nurture the children and harvest the crops, and our psyches are hard-wired to work in collectives. Men have had thousands of years to experiment with zeroing in on the kill. Now the shift of the ages begs the new paradigm of shared vision and manifestation where nobody succeeds unless all succeed. The woman's perspective finally has a spot in the marketplace, where women and men alike can take advantage of this more cooperative model.

Taking on a new power base after it has inadvertently been given over to others for centuries is a mind-expanding and truly powerful shift for women to make.

But I also see an overriding tendency to fall into "overwhelm and confusion" especially if a woman is attempting to move forward in her entrepreneurial business. Even with small children in the home, there are plenty of success stories of women managing to get a service-based business up and running that generates money for the family. It is, however, easy to be overcome by all of the many details in creating and organizing the business and prioritizing the myriad things to do.

Spinning one's wheels and really not getting anything accomplished is a real possibility as is the inevitable feeling of exhaustion and being overwhelmed.

The clutter and confusion mounts, and the poor woman is left feeling fatigued, hopeless, and in failure.

What to do? Again, start where you are. There is always a bit of time to take for oneself and go quietly within to listen carefully to what is actually happening. By listening to your intuition, you will generally come up with the right answer within the first two to three seconds of asking the question. Anything after that will likely be your mind wiggling in to make up something that sounds right but be overlaid with a story about the situation that is not your truthful, intuitive message.

This is the cornerstone of my coaching work with women who are on the verge of producing a new business based on the visions they see. They are coming into clarity and power with more purpose and waking up to the deeper possibilities of their true hearts' desires: not taking "impossible" for an answer. They are breaking through long-held invisible barriers to their potential and starting to manifest from that vision. There is a learning curve here, so be patient with your listening, and give yourself time to learn what is true information coming to you and what is false.

Building the intuition muscle takes time. At first, you must consciously plant the seed of knowing that your heart is speaking to you and you can listen, whether in the form of sensing your own gut instincts or cultivating an awareness of hearing, seeing, sensing, or knowing the subtle qualities and information coming to you. It is a "soulful listening" that you are cultivating.

Listen to your inner knowing and be willing to tell yourself the truth. You might have to go through a period of adjustment because there will also be a deep recognition dawning as to how much self-deception you have engaged in to protect yourself from pain. But getting your life back and activating your power will be so worthwhile that you become willing to take the risk of discomfort. And then you will be willing to take the time to figure out that your guidance has been ready to help you all along.

You are coming fully alive within as you settle down into your inner listening. You are being guided in new directions that may seem very unfamiliar to you. It may never have occurred to you that you can use this resource to guide you in starting a business and taking leadership of it.

The voice starts to give you messages and images about exactly what you need to do. It may not make sense to your linear mind, but creativity never works in a linear direction anyway; you are learning a new skill for how to live your life! You must first accept yourself, believe in yourself, and get your acceptance and likability from yourself instead of looking for approval from others. Then you are on your way to big things.

You start to rely on this information source as your trusted ally. You are reaching down into your creativity and drawing out the pearls that will create the string that is the coherent necklace for you to wear proudly in your new creation. You are creating something from nothing, simply because that something wants to take form and emerge in the world. Whether it is a piece of art, a service you offer, or an enterprise, it has begun from the depths of your creative impulse to participate and to belong as a player in the spirit of increase: the way the world was meant to thrive.

There is another thing that I want to bring to light in the creation stage of your new idea and that is to stay in a witnessing frame of mind. In life, and particularly when you are trying something new, there are only the old ways of interpreting information and experience you have to draw on. If you can stay in an attitude of witnessing without interpreting, you will be better off than if you have a ready interpretation about the "meaning" of what is happening as it unfolds.

Things do take an organic course in which your flexibility is important. You must develop a thick skin, especially if you are prone to talking to other people about what you want to create. Inevitably, you will be presented with their fears and their ideas of your capabilities. Your

vision could get easily diluted or derailed by their input, so protect your fledgling business while it is taking hold. Spring is a soft season for a reason. Plants emerge delicately from the ground after a lot of preparation and cultivation. We will speak more about this later, but, meanwhile, take great care about to whom you speak about your vision.

You may find that your loved ones aren't quite as supportive of you in your new endeavor as you thought they might be. You have rocked their boats. You have presented something that is not only out of your comfort zone but also out of their comfort zone; whatever advice they give you will be colored by their own habits and fears about you and how that affects them.

The overriding problem for humans is that we all have a strong ego structure, which is locked into the subconscious mind and is doing its job to keep us safe and keep us small so that we don't do anything dangerous. Change takes place against all odds, with careful attention and conscious determination.

Building a new business with all of the unknowns is the epitome of scary and dangerous. For instance a spouse may only be thinking in terms of how much this new idea

is going to drain your shared bank account. I have definitely experienced this one and the truth is, they are right! At first there will be more money going out than coming back in and perhaps your spouse knows you well enough to have some concrete concerns that you may not be spending your time in taking action that will result in actual revenue-generating activities.

But the good news is that past behavior does not predict future results. That is if you have the very best intention to make your dream business a reality by taking action, it will blossom. It has to! It is you who must really step up and believe in your potential and speak up loud and proud for what you are creating in a way that people understand what you are offering. You learn to ask for the business and do the appropriate sales and the marketing with clarity and determination in a way that your potential clients say "Yes, this is what I want!"

Being in business for yourself is a spiritual workshop and carries a huge learning curve, especially if you have only ever worked for someone else in the past. Shifting into being a business owner is hard work on a variety of levels. It requires you to shift your mindset and become the person who can make all of this happen. So, in the meantime, perhaps it is better to keep your new ideas and plans under wraps and spend your time carefully putting in place all the elements necessary to get the business on a successful track until you have your support firmly behind you. What you share with your significant other comes with a warning; it is probably better to first share your vision and ideas with your assistant or best friend before your life partner.

To observe things accurately as they are unfolding and make decisions about how to course-correct as needed is the path of the wise woman.

Be willing to observe instead of interpret, and keep going. Give yourself the encouragement you need on a daily basis by moving forward first with revenue-generating activities; get some money in your coffers! And of course, keep dreaming big.

Chapter Two: Radical Self-Care: Be Your Own Best Friend

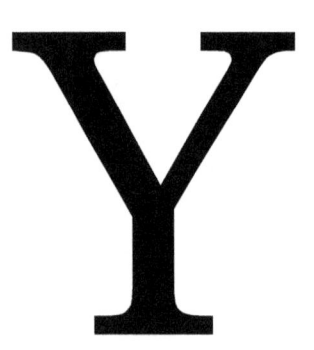

Yes, learn to be your own best friend! Whether your dream is lifestyle or business related, the practice of self-care is paramount. First, it will ensure that you are actually having fun along the way and not getting too stressed. Second, by putting into place platinum practices for self-care, you are creating a work-life balance that will serve all areas of your life, not just your business.

There are a lot of unhappy people walking around this world. We make assumptions that rich people are happy and that really successful people have it made, but that may not be true. You don't really know the quality of another person's life. What makes for a happy person, really? My definition of a happy person is one who is consciously choosing in every moment what is best for her, being loving and kind to others, and maintaining a divine balance in every aspect of her life. Most of all her happiness is also connected to meaning.

She is "healthy, wealthy, and wise." She is using all her gifts and talents in support of a balanced and abundance-driven life, and she is helping others through her good work. She has systems in place to make her business and life peaceful, and she has the support she needs to really thrive from her loved ones and her team. She has enough money not to feel concerned about bills and more than enough money to help others who are not so fortunate. She is creating a legacy that will live on beyond her that supports and helps to heal the planet.

We can be very far from that goal and still have it as an ideal in our mind's eye and be working toward it. In fact, it is really important to make long-term goals that are connected to the biggest vision possible for our dreams.

People who connect their goals to their most valued desires are crafting a big "why," a reason to go through the trouble of creating a business in the first place!

Key Number 2 is radical self-care. There are many elements in radical self-care that need to be put in place right from the beginning. This will ensure that while going after your dream you are also taking good care of yourself and your well-being. First and foremost is physical and emotional self-care.

What kinds of healthy practices do you have around food, sleep, and exercise? Have you cleansed all addictions out of your life so you are basically living in balance and only indulge your guilty pleasures once in a while? Are you enjoying a truly healthy life? Are you getting enough water, enough rest? Have you achieved your most comfortable weight? If not, what resources and practices can you put in place now that will bring you closer to your desired goal in six months, one year?

I have tremendous empathy for anyone struggling with weight. Believe me I know all about the weight thing. When I first moved to New York I was probably ten pounds overweight from a dancer's point of view. I believed that my dance teacher did not take me seriously because I didn't have the ideal ballet body that was the norm. This may not have been true, but I lived with the belief and was very hard on myself for years because of it.

I really struggled with my weight, and although I was working very hard and in extremely good shape, those extra pounds may as well have been hundreds of pounds of emotional weight that I carried with me. My self-image suffered immensely, and I rarely felt good about myself. I am not sure what others saw, but my anorexic mind only saw the flaws.

Slowly, over many years, I came into balance with my body, more because I was able to lose even more weight but mostly because I came to terms with my body image and was able to create and dance my choreography successfully; however, the internal judgments were always activated.

I wish that I could have understood then how valuable my sense of well-being has to come from me no matter what the external conditions; beauty exists deeply within our psyches. Girls, especially, have suffered in our culture from not being "good enough, pretty enough, thin enough": impossible standards for a young woman to come to terms with.

 Of course, this model of beauty has also been supported by a very aggressive advertising industry whose only true purpose is to sell products to unsuspecting women while their inner sense of worth and beauty goes through a dark, dark tunnel: "comparing and despairing."

Health is a great deal more than weight and appearance. Feeling healthy and happy is a very individual experience; be kind to yourself when it comes to your looks. You are beautiful and you are valuable. You are unique. There is literally nobody else in the world like you. You are an expression of God/Spirit's light in the world.

Creating a balanced mind/body harmony takes focus and commitment for the long term. Diet changes happen by listening to what your body needs over a time. If you listen carefully, your intuition will let you know what your body requires and what it doesn't. I am always amazed at what kinds of cravings—such as spinach, potato chips, orange juice, meat—that I desire at different times. I listen to those intuitions and fulfill them but not by over-indulging.

If I want a piece of chocolate cake it is because of a celebration of some kind, and I allow the celebratory experience to prevail; I eat a very modest portion while appreciating every delicious bite.

I believe this to be the secret of my success to being a size 6 at 60 years of age. And it can work for you too. I am very sad about how women judge themselves about the pounds they cannot shed, but this way of listening to the body and honoring your emotions is the very best path to losing the weight.

The delicate balance of your body's changing chemistry, as well as the nuanced nutritional shifts the body goes through on a daily basis, is so complex that we could never understand the components; however, our bodies are letting us know through the cravings and thoughts that appear regularly. Listen to your body with love and respect and nonjudgmentally, and you will find your weight coming into balance. You may also discover other subtle changes coming into your awareness as you bring renewed energy and balance into your life through your attention and awareness.

What is your body calling you to pay attention to? Where is the disharmony? What would you have to awaken within your conscious awareness to get it back in alignment, and what is the marker you use for being in alignment? In asking these questions, we are reaching within to uncover the source of peace and well-being. It is no less than the expression of your happiness, an internal description of your state of health and wellness.

This path is found through deep and careful attention to your own body, to your own rhythms, and especially to what pulls you off center. When you are well, there is a sense of flow within where your movement and breath and poise are all working effortlessly and beautifully. You are embodying an expanded and energetic version of your wholeness and you are experiencing yourself holistically. Your energy shines from the inside out, and you become magnetic. As you highlight the pursuit of the consciousness and desire to move always in the direction of harmony and well-being, the body aligns with your intentions.

This is about aligning with your true center and being very mindful about what you wanting and need for wholeness. Because food can be such a huge detractor from your health, we focus here very intentionally and listen to what happens in your body when you eat foods that don't agree with you.

There are also other self-care practices that work with your emotional health and well-being to support the process of consistent alignment. For instance, do you take time each morning to write in a journal? This simple activity done consistently begins to help you listen for what you want more of, and it gives you the authority to listen to your own voice first every day, before other people have a chance to interject their ideas.

Could you carve out a few minutes to write the intention you have for your day? What would you like to see happen today if you had the best- case scenario? State it in the positive, as though it is already on its way to you. You are creating a supportive environment that will draw to you more of what you want and less of what you don't want.

The power in the Law of Attraction, a basic law found in Nature, is aligned with the principle that "everything like unto itself is drawn." As like attracts like, the more you address and state what it is that you want, and not think too much of what you do not want, the principle activated will manifest the idea and an expression of the idea. You are participating in the activation of a future that is more in harmony with your wishes, and you begin releasing thoughts and patterns that are not aligned with your desires.

Over time the old memories of negative thinking and acting will fall away and you will see how much manifesting power you really do have. This works also for long-term goals. You may not have a clue as to how your desire will become a reality or how it could possibly appear in your life but as you draw the picture and visualize the qualities you want you are attracting a vision for what you are asking. This then activates your subconscious mind to bring in the people and circumstances to make it a reality too.

Spend most of your thoughts and energy focusing on what you want. Do you want more vibrant energy, more peace throughout your day? Think about practices you can do for yourself that bring refined energy and peace toward that end. If you want ease but spend your time running after every little email and phone message or trying to fulfill other people's needs, I can guarantee that you will not be feeling more energy and more peace.

You actually have to build the peace "muscle." Have you ever known people who actually live peacefully? I have. They are extraordinary people to be around because we slow down just being in their presence.

Clearly, it is a choice we all have available to us. Imagine going through an entire day in conscious awareness and peacefulness.

Why do we not choose this? I believe it is because there is a deeper and more pressing emotional dissonance working within, one that is wrought with negative self-talk, worry, doubt, and fear. Our ability not to listen to those inner voices that are leading us into positions of weakness and worry will slowly dissipate if we allow the deeper desires for peace and well-being to take over. It is simply a choice. How are you choosing to live?

One practice that has become very important to me is something I learned from my coach training with Sharon Wilson called "Belief Transformation." For this practice, you will need to place a piece of blank paper horizontally (the long part left to right). You begin by drawing four lines lengthwise down the paper. In the first column, write: "beliefs serving me"; in the second, "beliefs not serving me so well."

In the third column, identify and write out the belief triggering you the most from the second column; in the fourth column, write a "progressive belief" (for example, you could say "I want to believe that someday this will not be an issue for me"), then, the final column, write an action step you could take. Leave this column blank if you cannot think of one at the moment.

Now, the trick is to remember to write down your progressive belief every day. Over time, you will notice the wording begin to change. For a while it might look like "I want to believe that someday I will feel comfortable with technology," and then it might start to morph into "I do believe that technology is easy for me, but I need more support than I have right now."

I actually did this particular belief transformation over a period of months, and because I was so focused on changing the energy of my beliefs around technology, I found myself writing one day, "I believe that technology is easy for me, and, if ever I get tripped up, people will come bounding to my door to help me!" And one day my computer technology guy rang my doorbell just at the moment I needed help.

I was shifting the energy through this writing practice, and look what happened for me! This is positive evidence if I have ever seen it. So don't let this energy-management gem pass you by. This little template can move your consciousness to new heights. (I want to thank

Sharon Wilson for giving me this energy management tool. It alone has shifted my subconscious patterns and belief systems more than any other.) You can find it at: www.healingintoabundance.com/resources.

We all have beliefs that do not serve us in life, and it is often very difficult to get a handle on them because they are so deeply rooted in our subconscious minds. As you systematically begin to shift a belief day after day, you will see incremental changes that, over time, can create huge breakthroughs. This little practice is well worth bringing into your daily self-care practice, but it needs some time so make sure you carve out a few minutes every morning to do it. And don't just write out one belief. Work with eight to ten beliefs at a time, and see how your life changes for the better.

We dip into a more magical world when we begin to align with what we are wanting instead of with the pessimistic, determinist, negative voices in our minds. I believe in this practice so much that I am convinced people could pull themselves out of poverty and change the course of their lives if they created a disciplined approach to writing belief transformations. Most of what manifests outwardly comes directly from our inner thoughts, attitudes, and beliefs. As you shift your beliefs, many other things fall nicely into place to assist your success.

After you have done your journal writing and your belief transformation exercise, find a way to revisit some of your intentions during the day and see if what you are asking for is fulfilled through a "positive evidence." "Positive evidence" is anything that fulfills the desired intention. It could be that you heard something on the radio that supported your desire or you see a billboard as you are driving down the street that indicates an answer to a question that surfaced for you. It could be reading something later in the day that seems to be an answer to the question or desire you had.

"Positive evidences" are another name for what the great 20th-century psychologist Carl Jung called synchronicities. I think of them as little magical experiences we experience in our daily life that prove we are in right alignment with the Universe. The more we are able to live from a state of synchronicity and grace, the more joy and possibility enters our world. This is a good thing!

On the other hand, when our thoughts turn dark with negative images and ideas, or when we project these thoughts onto other people, we are, in effect, creating a heavy slate from which to function, and we will undoubtedly see all kinds of difficult situations emerge.

Yes, we have that much power to create either good or bad. The energy follows the thought and we are always creating. Have you ever heard the saying "how you do anything is how you do everything"? This shows you how powerful your intentions are and how the energy you expend in the delivery of a thought leads to an action. This follows another universal law: the law of Cause and Effect.

Generally, we are running from effect to effect in our lives, without a clue as to the cause that was put in place somewhere along the way. As you take back the responsibility for the cause itself, and choose to live from cause instead of effects, you regain the power to invest in the kinds of activities that will really help you turn your life and business toward the direction you want it to go.

Why not direct your thoughts in the direction of desire, purpose, and dreams so that there is a creative impulse working through you for your good and the good of those whom you encounter? The power of your intentions can be cultivated on a daily basis, helping you to separate your desires from those activities with which you would rather not participate.

Another practice for radical self-care lies in the arena of movement. Similar to how you can manage your weight and diet, there is an important quality that we need to enliven in life: to move and be moved. As a living, breathing creature, a woman needs to dance and laugh and cry and make love and be free to express herself. Moving your body, either in a structured way through exercise or in a less structured way such as walking and dancing, will make you much happier in the long run. So schedule into your daily routine some time to move, breathe, and shall I say...dance!

I am a born dancer. When I was a little girl, I told my mother I wanted to be a ballerina when I grew up. I had a music box with a tiny figurine of a ballet dancer in a long pink tutu that moved in a circle if I wound up the mechanical key, and I would watch her circle around and around. Although I never actually attended a ballet until I was much older, this little dancer captured my imagination for hours at a time.

If you ever watch children playing, you will see that their curiosity is always moving them to run, play, squeal, wiggle, adapt, and explore. They make forts, climb fences, and generally use their bodies to full capacity all day long.

What happens when we get older? Why do we stop moving and exploring the way we did as young children? And worse, how do we forget to move altogether as time goes by? The better question is: what would it take to bring some of that movement back into our lives?

Try this exercise right now. Go find your favorite music, something that you really love to dance to, and get up and move for a few minutes then sit back down and notice what feels different. Could you find a way to incorporate more movement or dance into your day? Notice if you are more tired after doing this activity or more invigorated.

There is a practice that I studied years ago called Authentic Movement, a formal activity with very simple rules. I would like to describe the process to you because it made such an impact on me, and you might want to try it for yourself.

You need to have at least two people participating. One is called the Witness and the other is called the Mover (with more than two people there continues to be one Mover and the rest are Witnesses, but you can change the rules any way you like). There is no music, only the voice of the Mover. The Mover starts with eyes closed and only moves if and when she is authentically called to move. The Witness observes without offering advice or comments. The two people decide beforehand how long the moving will go on. After the session, if the mover requests comments, the Witness offers comments but no evaluation. Then they switch roles and repeat in the same way.

This is sacred work. Seldom does the Mover not have an extraordinary experience. The process of being witnessed is an integral part of the experience. Clients have reported that my unique system for bringing in more "power and presence" has given them the confidence and critical edge they need to be ready to step into the spotlight and shine in their businesses!

To review: We have spoken about listening to what your body is telling you to eat; journaling to listen more power fully to your own inner voice; implementing more movement and dance to help keep you happy, healthy, and on purpose; and shifting your thoughts and negative self-talk to more fully embody the powerful person that you are. You get to be more in the driver's seat of your own life, creating a healthy environment in which to live. And you get to be authentically you in the process, bringing more play, movement, and dance into your life.

We also talked about getting enough sleep and drinking plenty of water throughout the day. The next thing is to give yourself loving care by bringing more beauty and pleasure into your life. Nature is a great place to start with beauty and pleasure. (Great sex will also open your second chakra, bring vibrancy to your energy, and balance your hormones, so keep that on your roster as well!)

I am lucky to live in a gorgeous city with a great deal of culture: music, dance, art museums, and libraries. Amplifying your "diet" of beautiful and stimulating opportunities for inspiration through the arts will enhance your self-care enormously. And if you can learn a musical instrument or take a dance class, even better. Reading and taking in inspirational material, whether it is from personal-development writers or the classics, will go a long way to bring more stimulation and inspiration into your life.

Try new things even if you have a preconceived notion that you will not like them. Get to know what it is that you really love and love to do; then let yourself be immersed in it. Organize your time so that the day doesn't get away from you before you have brought in a little of that spiritual food for yourself.

And last, some people are helped by a daily meditation or breathing practice. I love to meditate with other people. My start in meditation practice was with Zen Buddhism and then Tibetan Buddhism, so I am steeped in the language of mudra and mantra as a focus for the mind. But there are countless different ways to meditate. Prayer is also a form of meditation, although the focus is a bit different. Even listening to meditative music can act as a way to quiet the mind and reduce stress.

We will be speaking at great length about learning to use inner energy management techniques to manage stress and develop soul energy later in the book, so for the time being I will simply suggest that you find an easy way to quiet yourself on a daily basis whether through a formal meditation practice or merely taking a few minutes to close your eyes and tune in to your heart. It will do wonders for bringing a refreshed spirit to your activities. Once you develop the discipline for this, you will always cherish it as your number-one resource for inner contentment. Then nobody can ever really throw you off balance. Your inner alignment will be rock solid, and you will bask in the contentment of a life in which you consistently connect with others but keep your own counsel, where you feel safe to let your love out but keep your spirituality deep inside and private.

Chapter Three: Inner Energy Practices for Calm, Confident Focus

So what is Energy Management? Do you manage your energy, or is your energy flying off the handle and sending you down rabbit holes? If you are not consciously managing your energy, your lack of energy management may be managing you. And that is not a pretty picture!

Have you ever gone through an entire day putting out fires and feeling that you were two steps behind? I know I have. This looks like you just can't get a handle on your time, your energy, the tasks you have to complete, or you are having trouble reaching those people with whom you are meant to connect.

You are in struggle the whole time. You are stressed, overwhelmed, exhausted, and not getting anything done. Then the confusion sets in, along with feelings of frustration or even defeat. Your energy wanes more, and you are ready to give up, but something else happens that requires too much of your depleted energy, and then you just lose it.

You want to scream, cry, take it out on someone else, or you just shut down and stop. You give up. Then after this, the negative voices will most likely have a field day with you. "I'll never get this, I'm a failure, what's the use, it's his or her fault." In effect, you have terrorized yourself.

Ah but there is a better way! Key Number 3 is learning simple, elegant inner energy-management practices that you can do every day. Let's backtrack just a little and see if the alignment that you were desperately wanting could come back to you. You have tools that you are not yet using because you don't know about them. You've already done the radical self-care but this is a task for the heavy artillery…your ability to activate your thoughts to immediately de-stress your body and the emotional charge that is surging through you..

Especially when you have fallen into this hole, you need to know that there is help internally. It comes completely from you and if used, things will get better.

Inner energy management tools are the tools you can use to stop in the moment where the tangled energy starts to present itself, and where you have something you can do or think that allows you to steer clear of the disaster and move in a different, less damaging direction.

It is a skill you build, and awareness you cultivate. This is why I call it a "practice." The ability you have to achieve a shift while you are going through a hard time only happens because you have prepared the ground before the big upset takes place. You have learned to manage your energy when the stakes weren't so high.

Let's say, for example, that you have to get an article completed for your newsletter, and your computer is not complying. You try over and over again to do the same task, but it is just not working. Before you waste too much time and end in a puddle of self-judgment and tears, just stop.

Tool Number 1 is to stop and not do anything. Breathe. Breathing turns out to be the go-to energy tool of all energy tools, because when under duress we all forget to breathe. So breathe. Then assess.

Sometimes the assessment is simply, "Oh my computer is not working. Hmmmm. Maybe the modem is down or the outside wire is down." Breathe again. Step two might be something like "Even though my computer is not working and I really want to get this done, maybe it doesn't have to be completed right now. Maybe I have time to call the Internet company, and let them help me." Good start.

You have to start talking to yourself and making some objective assessments. Maybe walk away from the project altogether for a while or even until the next day when you can get a fresh start. Maybe there is something else you can do to start feeling just a little bit better. Ask yourself "What is triggering me the most right now?" You might hit on something that you can untangle in the moment and go on. Or not. If not, there is more work to be done.

We are bringing logic into the situation. But more, we are listening for what is actually happening, something tangible that can be sensed in your body and that you can bring some light of understanding to mentally and emotionally, which might provide just enough clarity and space from the upset to bring you back into alignment with your desires for the bigger goal. Objectively speaking, it is not the end of the world to miss a day in writing your newsletter if something more important must be done first. The role of a CEO in your own business knows how to diffuse potentially destructive situations and move forward.

Upset breeds more upset, unfortunately. And its opposite, equanimity in the midst of chaos, brings a higher vibrational energy that you can draw on during times that would otherwise lend themselves to frustration.

Now frustration is not a terrible thing in the moment. A good healthy dose of anger could be the perfect antidote to pent-up frustration, so please don't judge your expression. Vocalizing may be just what is needed to release the trauma that has accumulated energetically during the episode. As a fledgling energy healer, you want to be able to recognize the trauma as it is settling into your system and have the tools for clearing it right away.

Your awareness is the key. Being aware of the feeling in the moment is extremely helpful but easily overlooked in the charge of the emotional reaction. The skill you are building is to pause in that moment and have something else you could do or think instead that would shift the energy into something a little more proactive. I call this "responding, not reacting."

Your response might ultimately be the very same choice as the reacting choice, but you have instituted an inhibitory moment of pausing first, which informed the choice! This gives you the power of a more appropriate response, if needed. It puts you in control as a generator instead of a reactor. This results in fewer fires to put out in the long run because you are shifting into assessment and choice as opposed to reaction.

You will start to use your mastery in these momentary setbacks and develop a mental muscle for using this awareness to enact change and release fear, trauma, frustration, and aggravation. This will make you more available to quickly reframe the experience to your advantage. Eventually, you can enjoy the fruits of your new level of mastery as a gentle shift from strain to ease in your thinking, feelings, and actions.

Other people can catalyze the same kinds of frustration and reaction in you, even well-meaning people like your children (who are only acting from the spontaneity of their exuberance at the very moment you have to write that critical email or article). As you work with your energy to absorb the excess drama and trauma that comes through the emotional body, you can meet the stimulus with calm assurance and get back on task quickly and effortlessly.

Designing your life while expecting some inevitable dissonance to show up throughout your day, and knowing how to take care of it in the moment, will encourage a deepening of the value you hold for yourself. You will see a greater sense of peace emerge. This builds upon itself. As you successfully meet the stimuli that set you wrong and down the rabbit hole of distress, you will gain confidence and mastery and have a new toolbox with which to manage other more difficult situations.

The self-care practice I have been describing is similar to what is currently called Mindfulness Meditation. Mindfulness, simply defined, is the ability to bring more conscious awareness to your activities. Mindfulness can be accessed easily through meditation but it can be accessed in other ways, too.

One of my favorite practices, and one I literally do first thing every morning, is a breathing meditation that I call the "whispered ah," which I received from my training to be an Alexander Technique teacher. The "whispered ah" can be done simply or it can be quite complex, but for our purposes, just walk through this practice with me, and you will experience a momentary pause in your day that can be extremely relaxing and nourishing. Here we go:

Sit quietly on a chair with both feet on the floor or sit in a cross-legged position on the floor. You can also lie down on a blanket on the floor with your knees bent and feet on the ground. You will also need a few soft-bound books to place under your head for support if you choose this position. In the Alexander Technique, we call this the "Active Rest" position, or semi-supine. Let your head gently ungrip from your neck and close your eyes. Let your spine stay elongated but not overly upright. Now just let the breath go out. You should feel your ribs move a little bit, like an umbrella closing gently. Now pause and don't allow an immediate new breath in just yet. Momentarily pause, and do nothing. You will automatically let a new breath come in at the right time, spontaneously, as though it was just bubbling up from nowhere.

This is your natural physiologic system doing what it is meant to do, which is to "breathe you." That's right; if you can leave yourself alone and pay attention to the gentle outbreath, the inbreath will take care of itself. You don't have to "take a breath." You are being breathed in the same way that you breathe when you are sleeping, only now you are bringing your awareness to the activity. Go ahead and continue with this process for ten to twenty breaths. When you are ready, simply breathe normally and go about your day.

Did you notice anything? Sometimes this process produces a spontaneous deep and released breath, as if you are letting go of some of the residual fatigue that you have been carrying around with you. This is all for your benefit and part of your stress-management plan.

Eventually, you will have the facility to do the "whispered ah" any time: when waiting for a light to change while driving, when someone is acting out of anger in front of you, when you cannot get to sleep; it is yours to use any time you need more calm.

I did say that the "whispered ah" can be more or less complex. What makes it more involved is when you also whisper an "ah" sound, which brings in the action of the jaw and the option to exhale while making a sound. Actors and singers have used this method for more than one hundred years to develop more sonorous beauty of the voice, and you can develop a better quality of voice, too, if you follow these instructions. Your confidence and command of the stage will grow in as you master the "whispered ah," a wonderful tool for developing a magnetic presence for public speaking and networking.

For now, just practice the basic awareness technique of noticing your exhalation while breathing, and extend it a little bit so that the new spontaneous inhale takes place naturally.

As you gain skill in this practice, you will gently begin to unravel tension patterns long held within your body, coming from excess tension and downward pulls on your upper back musculature, your diaphragm and your rib cage. Even chronically holding your stomach in can set up a negative breath-holding condition that becomes "normal" and causes huge imbalance and restrictions within your movement coordination, leading to poor posture and neck, back, and knee pain.

This simple practice of breathing with the intention of experiencing more release of the breath can go a long way toward better health and well- being.

Imagine having a real energy-management toolbox at your disposal. There are countless inner-energy management tools available for you in your toolbox. Don't leave home without it. You can learn to heighten your intuition, talk with your inner business manager, even receive guidance from spirit guides.

Sometimes referred to as your higher self, this is a part of your psyche that simply knows things. As you gain facility in using guided meditation and inner visioning, you will gain much peace of mind because you are listening to the wisdom you carry within, and you are making decisions for your business, relationships, and your life that are aligned and connected to what matters most to you.

As you draw on this guidance, you are, in essence, drawing closer to the meaning of your life. You will have the self-assurance that nobody can throw you off your game, and you will listen to your own counsel instead of relying on advice from other people.

Listening to your inner guidance and intuition is the most precious gift you can ever give yourself. Growing in awareness and consciousness will lead you onto the path of your soul's presence and purpose. You can seek and gain assistance from your own inner guidance and intuition so that the seemingly overwhelming aspects of running your business, family, and life don't get the best of you.

You have help from the inside. You can learn to listen to the signs that your body and your feelings are giving you about how to be in the present so that any need to address or fix a situation that doesn't feel quite right will come handily, and you become aware of new possibilities that had not occurred to you until the moment arose. Sometimes known as "flashes of insight," you can be trained to use your inner guidance system just like any other skill is mastered. It is an awareness that has been available to you all along but—for most of us—underappreciated and underused.

I trained myself to use my intuition when I was in my early twenties. I was drawn to Tarot as a symbol system for assessment, not so much for prediction, and I quickly became engrossed in it. The layers of meaning regarding the current circumstances of a person's life endlessly intrigued me, and as I became proficient in "reading the cards"; the person's past, present, future instinctively made sense to me. I used the cards as a starting place, but as I became confident in the intuitive skills I was developing, I became more comfortable sharing whatever was coming to mind to say to my client, and the value to them was recognized by both of us.

This encouraged me to go deeper, be more active in listening to my intuition and trusting and opening to a beautiful world of mystery and connectedness through opening to these intuitive gifts.

Anyone can do this if they want to learn. This skill comes through us as a channel of awareness, including the ability to see visions and pictures, sometimes to hear phrases or words that are significant for the one receiving the reading and sometimes just as a certainty, a deep knowing about the person's question or issue.

After some preliminary skill and knowledge building you can go on to master what I call the "four clairs": clairvoyance, clairaudience, clairsentience, and claircognizance.

Each of these "clairs" has a specific quality that gives you information about an event or experience that can be understood, enhanced, reclaimed, released, or revealed by using your intuition.

Usually we have one or two dominant "clairs" but all four of them can be developed, which will make you a more helpful assistant for people's distress. The world of energy and spiritual healing is simply the next logical step in your development. I was taught these skills, and you also can be taught. It opens your world to greater access and sense of involvement in the elegant and intangible aspects of your potential, so don't delay in receiving help here!

Energy Management and Intuition Development are core skills I teach all my high-performance coaching clients to learn to do for themselves. I consider this inner energy management work to be the core of your practices that bring greater clarity and energy to everything you do, and also open your intuition in a very real and tangible way.

What do you do on a daily basis to manage your energy? Do you have a systematic plan for up-leveling your energy every day? If not, you may notice that you aren't always in full control of your life, and you can feel life being challenging and difficult. You would then most likely be living in a reactive instead of proactive or interactive state.

This is not pleasant in the long run. You would be losing energy, which may lead to feeling less than empowered. You may be experiencing self-doubt or unworthiness, or you could feel yourself being a victim of life's happenings rather than a happy player in your own right, constantly running around putting out fires instead of being the proactive inventor of your creative energy. You could end up feeling like the frantic, busy person you never wanted to become: exhausted and out of alignment.

As you gently grow in the ways of energy management, you will start to see some changes in your life. You will have more energy to deal with the little things life throws your way; the inevitable troubles that come to everyone will not take such a toll on you. It is as if you have a little angel on your side, whispering into your ear: "go this way!" You begin to make better, more intuitive choices about what you should do to complete a project, what you could be doing to release a negative memory or getting proper help when you need it. The choice to make your inner world balanced and healthy, along with the tools to get you there, will go a long way in creating a business and life that is happy and flourishing in ways you never before dreamed possible.

And the secret bonus to making these shifts and gathering these tools is that you will be present to welcome opportunities that you never could have seen when your energy was low. This is because you are creating a high vibrational frequency that holds more energy and intensity, just as light is a higher vibration than sound. People are attracted to this energy, and your inner beauty and essence will show through more and more. People will see you, want what you have, and want to connect with you.

Here is a simple exercise: Sit quietly and let your breathing slow down. Let your feet come softly to the floor, and relax your belly. Drop your attention down into your hips, and then let the sitting bones release toward the chair. Take in the sounds of your environment but allow them to fall away quietly. Keep breathing in and out, and begin to think about something that happened recently for which you are grateful. It could be something really small: a child smiling at you, a nod from a friendly person on the street, a good meal, a warm and inviting home when it is cold outside. Really take that in for the moment. Notice how the thought and feeling lets you come more fully present to this moment.

Keep breathing in the gratitude, and now think of something else that you are grateful for. Connect with that feeling quietly, and breathe that in as well. You are coming up with a list of things that have brought you some joy, no matter how small.

Perhaps keep a journal of five things that you are grateful for each and every day. Don't make this a big deal; just jot down what these things are so that you can add to them daily. If daily is too much, have a "gratitude Friday" when, at the end of each week, you spend a bit of time remembering your good fortune, however small. You may notice a slight shift in your "joy" energy over time and that you can focus more on the good than the frustrations that emerge in your life. This is adding to your surplus of thoughtful and happy feelings and will start to shift some of the other more challenging events that accumulate during your day.

Eventually, you will be seen as the optimistic and powerful leader who shows up at every event, someone whom others rely upon to bring up the vibration of the group and add to the positive qualities of an event or meeting. Other things may start to show up as well: opportunities that were not usually present in the past, ideas that you can work with to create even more presence and power.

So let's talk about how to set up and choose your vibrant business using some of these energy-management tools. As you strengthen your resolve to live a peaceful, exciting life, you are already one giant step closer to your goals. As you simply show up and say "yes" to your future self, I will guarantee that things will start to open up for you. How do I know? It is one of the most basic spiritual laws: the Law of Increase.

To this end, the power of decision is huge. In writing the book <u>Think and Grow Rich</u> (Penguin Books 2003, originally published in 1937; Ralston Society), Napoleon Hill interviewed 500 of the most highly productive and successful people of the age. Virtually all of them made decisions quickly and changed their minds slowly if at all. On the other hand, nonproductive people tended to make decisions slowly and change their minds frequently, showing that the skill of decision making is paramount to creating a powerful platform from which to live one's life.

If you are not one who makes decisions quickly, what can you do to start to change that behavior? Let's say that you had the opportunity to take a year-long Mastermind (generally recognized as a group coaching program with a mentor and other like-minded individuals who share the same values and wish to develop skill and be accountable for the goals they make). Your first impulse may be to say "I don't have the money for that," but what may be underlying your immediate thought is a deeper fear that you don't have what it takes to do the work; therefore, you default to the idea that you can't afford it. Money becomes your catchall excuse for staying where you are and not moving through the discomfort of changing your attitudes and habits and ultimately having the joy and success you deserve.

What if, instead, you made a decision that you don't want things to continue going along the same track you have always been on? What if, even if you don't know exactly what is going to happen or whether you will succeed, you are willing to consciously choose the change and take a risk, go ahead, and say "yes" to the opportunity?

The people that Napoleon Hill interviewed were the men building the banks and the railroads in the early 20th century, the businessmen who had ideas for companies that had never yet existed, all this during the biggest depression that America had ever endured. They said yes to opportunities that didn't look like opportunities at all. In fact, what they were taking a chance on made no logical sense, but there was something in their characters that allowed them to take a risk and say yes without hesitating or backtracking.

The stakes aren't nearly as high today. Although the markets swing wildly, and you may have experienced some real hardship, there is always a way to turn things around, but you have to have the courage and willingness to make a change that doesn't make sense according to your bank balance. It does, however, make sense for your business because you don't exist in a vacuum, and you are not supposed to do everything on your own, especially without prior knowledge.

Your coach/mentor most likely has done all this before you so you don't have to reinvent the wheel. You can ride on the wisdom and knowledge of someone who can guide you and lead you toward your dream and steer you away from the deadends. You will see changes in your income, your impact, and your sense of accomplishment and well-being.

I know this first hand from my mentor. Like me, she has a big dream for herself. She is gracious and spiritual. She has paid her dues by spending the same money on her own learning that she is asking me to spend. I have learned from her advice, especially of what not to do, so I can move forward faster and with much less self-doubt and confusion. Why not give yourself the same advantage?

It is a decision, nothing more. As you say yes to the possibilities that are unfolding in front of you, all manner of things line up in your favor to help you succeed. That's how the Universe works. It is abundant, willing, and ready to assist you in all that you do. How do I know this? The Universal Law of Increase springs into effect when and to the extent that you use it.

So, to review: We started this chapter with a discussion of energy- management principles, as though you had a tool box at your disposal that can help you manage and up-level your vibrational frequency any time you want to take advantage of it.

Much of this work is learning to use your own inner guidance, which is available to you 24/7. You can bring awareness to yourself when you start to feel anxious or irritated and stop in the moment the stimulus is beginning to affect you. You can release the trauma immediately by knowing how to clear the energy.

You can start the dual practices of belief transformation and gratitude on a regular basis to remember all that life has given you and recognize that you already have much abundance and are playing in a field of overflow.

You can develop a platinum practice of sitting quietly every morning and meditating before writing in a journal, doing some "whispered ah" cycles, and setting your intention for what it is that you are most wanting for the day. This is a way of speaking to the Universe and saying "this is how I want things to go for me today." You say, "I want peace and excitement and ease. I want vibrancy and flow. I want a perfect outcome for the tasks that I need to do to accomplish both my short- and long-term goals. I am ready and willing to make the decision to move forward with consciousness and stand by my choices. I am willing to be accountable for what it is that I say I want."

Then, if something comes out of the blue to cause some stress, you will be ready to counter the energy with your deeper convictions and know how to meet the stimulus with calm abiding.

Even if you get totally derailed, there is always a good night's sleep and a new day tomorrow. Don't think lightly of the dreamtime. Many conundrums have been solved by "sleeping on it." In sleep, our subconscious mind can play and give us answers that were unknown to us when the problem arose. Even Albert Einstein used this tactic for his problem solving.

My favorite energy-management tool of all is the Belief Transformation Tool. Please go to my Website to download a FREE report that takes you through this important process: www.creativitywellspeing.com/resources.

The creative mind knows no limits. The only limits we put upon ourselves are those habitual patterns, stories, and behaviors that we perpetuate because they feel normal to us. If you really had the option to release lack, scarcity, fear, awkwardness, and doubt, would you be holding on to all those stories? Probably not. It is simply that you have not yet received enough quality information to make a change.

The wisdom for taking action in all this is "baby steps." Do just one little movement toward your goal today. Ask you inner guidance what the perfect next step is for you, and don't worry about the rest. Move out in faith, and know that things will unfold for you because you took an active step toward your heart's desire.

The famous Nike quote "just do it" has some profound advice for us. What is the worst that could happen? You might fall on your butt. So OK. Then get up, and take another step!

Chapter Four: How to Clear the Clutter, Simplify, and Envision Your Dream

"And the day came when the risk to remain tight in a bud was more painful than the risk it took to blossom."

Anais Nin

Nature gives us all the clues we need for a life well lived. Nature shows us that life unfolds before us naturally, inevitably. There is no question about the next step in nature. The bud has to grow into the flower. The flower has to share its fragrance. And then it inevitably has to fall gently to the ground. And so the cycle goes.

For us it is the same. Putting one foot forward and taking a step toward our desires is the first and only thing to do. Say yes to your desires regarding who you are and what you want fearlessly, with enthusiasm and conviction, without worry or doubt, without second-guessing yourself. And know in your heart that you deserve to be right here consciously choosing and doing your dharma.

The word "dharma" comes from Tibetan Buddhism and means your true work or your life's path. To do your dharma is to live authentically in the way you are meant to, according to the deeper purpose with which you have been assigned. Call it the momentum path of your soul's evolution, something within that drives you forward with intention and intensity, with passion.

Anais held her life up to the kind of dharmic scrutiny of which I am speaking. I met Anais Nin in the late seventies when I was in college. She was in her eighties then and exquisitely beautiful. She had her white hair tied in a knot behind her head and was wearing a tailored grey wool suit that day. Then she proceeded to read the raciest passage from one of her diaries! I was mesmerized. She was fully self-expressed and a model for those of us who did not yet own our voices. She did not let life or societal norms and behaviors censor her. She was her own woman and therefore a role model: contemporary goddess for us.

So take the step. Key Number 4 is to clear the clutter of your life and get really clear on your vision. This means it is OK to go slowly and put one foot in front of the other. Rome wasn't built in a day. You weren't created in a day. Take your time and you will be so happy when you see the result of your cumulative efforts. But take the step in the right direction for you so as not to walk headlong in the wrong direction. How many people do you know who have done an entire graduate program in a subject that later they find out they have no interest? The first step must be in the direction of your dreams and heart's desires. Sometimes it takes great searching and introspection to know what that is for you.

You must prepare the ground before you can sprout your new creation. If you have ever watched farmers ready the soil for the new planting, you will know what I mean. Usually after trial and error, and having had less than stellar harvests, farmers learn the skills of preparing the

ground. The conditions of their particular soil must be observed and tested. Then the proper combination of chemistry in the way of nutrients for the soil must be studied and combined.

They would have to go out and find the correct ingredients, then bring them home and mix them until they have the perfect combination for the specific food they are planting. Then they turn these nutrients into the existing soil. And, only then, the soil is ready for planting.

Even before the planting the farmers have most likely created small boxes of earth and planted the seedlings carefully and in the proper conditions and temperature so that, at the perfect time, the conditions are optimal for the little plantlets to be placed into the ground.

And then they must continue to nurture, water and weed without seeing much result. They have done all this on the promise that their plantings will bear fruit.

And finally they bloom. The tiny leaves emerge, then the flowers, and— finally—the actual vegetable or herb. Even then, the garden must be continuously fed and nurtured so that the food can be eventually harvested and consumed.

It is much like this for you and your fledgling business. You have an idea, a passion that must be carefully nurtured. You might not even share it with others at first for fear of some misguided friend or partner trampling on it before it can take root.

What if you don't even know what the first or next step is: you only know that you have a vision? Your dream needs to be cared for, and you must be able to hold that vision for a long time, if necessary. You may still be in a full-time job and not enough time or money to invest now. You might be feeling stuck and not knowing which direction to go to make your vision a reality.

You might not know how to articulate what it is that you want to create because it is only still just an impulse within you or a restless feeling. You might need to gain skills that you don't yet have.

This is where the soul's map comes in. Connecting with your own fledgling soul-full desire is the number one most valuable, most important thing you can do. Quiet down until you know, in your heart of hearts, what your soul desires. Sit before a blank piece of paper and just breathe for a while before you begin to write your vision. Hold that soft place within your being: fully at first, before there are even words. If you take the time to plant your seeds with all of the tenderness of the farmer, your soul-inspired vision will emerge as a fledgling idea. It will take its place in the world as if it had always been there.

When you light a candle, the flame rises up. It doesn't just smolder. You have to bring your attention and love to it and get the extra wax away from the wick and sometimes tenderly blow on it but eventually it ignites, breathing in the surrounding oxygen and making light. And so your work is done. You have facilitated light for the room.

The creative process is much like this. Often experienced as a yearning that holds an emotional edge but not much more, it is your conscious intention that brings it to life. Take the time to find out what kind of soil is needed, what conditions you must create. Begin in the present by really looking at the desire you have with simple observation so that you can start to bring it into form. This is a sacred process of manifestation. It is your baby, your dream.

The first step is usually to create an outline of what you want to produce. What does it look like if you could just dream about it? Who would you be if it was already in place? Do you have employees? Are you in a physical office? If so, how is it decorated? Are you working from home? What does your environment look like?

If you could give it a name right now, what would it be? Don't worry; you can change it along the way. This just gives you a way to envision and play. Later you can refine it, add to it, and throw out some of the ideas that don't fit. For now, you just want to begin making it real in your own mind.

Let's do another exercise:

Let's envision your perfect day. Close your eyes, and take a few deep, cleansing breaths. Settle into yourself, and feel your belly moving with your breath. Let your shoulders soften a little, and let your neck lengthen and release. Maybe allow your head to nod forward just a little bit without dropping into your chest. Listen to your body and what it might need right now.

Let your legs release downward toward the floor, and imagine yourself being held by the chair and by the Earth under you.

We are going to begin to imagine together what a perfect day would look like for you. How do you awaken in the morning? What do you see, hear, smell, and feel in your body? Imagine yourself being led by something that really excites you. Where are you going, and what are you thinking? See the day unfolding perfectly with joy and abandon.

Notice who is with you and why you feel so good with them.

What are you doing? Even more, what are you creating? What projects or activities are you engaged in? Take some time now, and really imagine your day. What would you have done by the end of the day? What project or tale would you talk about to someone else?

Take your time and really dream this day all the way to the end when you are going to bed and reflecting on what happened in a perfect way. Let yourself bask in the joy and freedom and satisfaction of this.

Then slowly, and only when you are ready, open your eyes and come back to yourself, your body, and your breathing. Then take a few minutes to write down any thing that you would like to remember about the experience.

So what would it take to make this day a reality in your life? Without changing the state you are in, allow this perfect experience to flood your mind with possibility and know that when there is an idea, when you can clearly see a vision, that the vision on some level already exists within you, and you have the capacity to make it real.

Then, after some time really living in the possibility of this heart's dream, let yourself decide that you actually want it. Make a decision right now that you can have this dream and that it belongs to you.

Remember that we already spoke about you being your own best friend in your radical self-care? Well, you are going to use that knowledge and truth about yourself to begin to call in this new reality one baby step at a time. You are going to choose it over and over again. You are also going to choose not to follow the negative voices that will inevitably come up to tell you that you can't have it.

This is where your conviction has to be really strong because if you don't talk yourself out of your vision, you can bet that someone will do it for you! We all survive on "same ol', same ol'" which is another way of saying we like things the way they are. We don't want any big, scary changes in our lives. In fact, the older we get the more our dreams don't come true because we gather a pack of excuses that keep us exactly where we have been. Why? Because that feels safe to us. The ego is a part of our psyche whose job it is to "just keep things the way they are, don't make any changes."

This is, of course, the reason you don't get beyond your initial vision. It is also the reason you want to hold onto the past. This includes your environment and the choices you make to keep you from diving in to your dreams. Even baby steps seem insurmountable from this point of view. There won't be any forward movement because your whole being is saying, "NO, not yet, I'm not ready!!"

So we have a bit of a project ahead of us if manifesting your vision is a real possibility for you. You have to stop riding the bike with the brakes on. You have to stop letting the fear, the excuses, and the uncomfortable unknown get to you.

The great innovator, F.M Alexander, who created the worldwide educational method—The Alexander Technique—developed his mind/body transformation method on this precise problem. He helped countless people

change the way they held tension in their bodies by understanding this point about ourselves. We are so afraid to change habits and patterns, and so unaware of them, that we don't change, and they get worse. We move awkwardly, develop all kinds of pain syndromes, and lose our natural poise and uprightness, all because the habits feel normal to us. Thus, we are unlikely to want to move bravely forward into the unknown territory of trying to move differently because it simply doesn't feel right.

Mr. Alexander was a careful observer and was able to recognize the problem and create a method for change that specifically recognized the habit itself as the problem. With this knowledge as the foundational basis for change, he then carefully crafted a psychophysical process through which to change habits.

If you would take the time and have the patience to go through this process, the result is an improved physical and emotional experience of well-being. Countless benefits result: less physical tension, improved coordination of movement, more poise and presence, visible grace, and better response to all stimuli.

These results would help you feel better physically and have more confidence, more command and power in your

interactions with others, a great deal more personal elegance, and heightened self-awareness.

You learn a skill for meeting any stimulus that you encounter from the stresses of ordinary life to creating a life and business of your dreams and having the emotional equipment necessary help you create what it is that you say you want.

There are just some minor things in the way: for example, a pervasive attitude that you can't have it! Although the true reasons for this attitude often lie in your subconscious beliefs about limitation and lack that may not even belong to you, the excuses sound more like "I don't have the time; I don't have the money right now to get the coaching; the timing isn't right; my husband/wife/father won't let me pursue my dreams because I have spent too much money on them in the past." How do I know this? They have all been my excuses at one time or another.

This is a crafty way for your own mind to keep the brakes on so that you never have to change or grow, and it will be the reason why you end up being in the same place that you are in now, one year, two years down the road. Your dreams will keep drifting down the road of the future until the dream is smothered like the end of a warm fire: dying embers down to the ashes.

What to do instead? Look around you. Look at your home, your office, the things you keep in your room. How organized are you? What commitments do you keep, and what do you conveniently forget about? Do you do what you say you are going to do? What stops you? Who do you forget to call back to follow through on networking, and where do those little notes to yourself get lost? And whom are you blaming for this?

Whew! Not to worry; I can help you get through this. I am well qualified because I am guilty of each and every one of the things I just listed. It is now time to get organized! It is now time to really come clean with yourself and make some changes in your work and home environment. It is time to create systems so that you don't have to work so hard and don't have to remember everything on your own.

Coaching consists of two main things: inner mindset work to change old behaviors and strategizing, goal setting, and accountability to plan your course of action. Healing and taking action—usually in that order—although every step along your entrepreneurial path will be a weaving of the inner and the outer aspects of you in your business. We take the deep dive whenever something known or unknown to you is getting in the way, and we take consistent, practical and strategic action toward the goal, whatever it is.

Overwhelm is simply the inability to make forward movement toward your goals because there is too much information coming in without that balance of action going out. We have to look carefully into the dark corners of your procrastination and begin to baby-step through what is keeping you from making things happen.

You do deserve your dream. It just takes a little bit of loving attention.

We have already spent time with self-care and energy management, which offers a beautifully crafted support for your inner sense of empowered self-mastery. Now we will move on to carefully and lovingly organizing your time and space (environment). We will deal with these two

things separately. This can be very exciting work if you let yourself play with the devil. You know "the devil is in the details" right? You need support and you need sys tems to manage your business and life. Think of these two elements as your very own personal manager.

Hopefully, you can get a real personal manager soon if you don't already have one. Today we call these people virtual assistants, whom you hire through the Internet at a mutually agreed upon number of hours to help the back end of your business. The world of business changed when virtual assistants came on the scene. They do the things that you aren't good at or that you would prefer not to do: organize your planner, format your newsletter, then on to the more complex activities of making cold calls for potential speaking opportunities and setting up your video conferences. Then there is the dreaded technological work; do you really think you are well served to spend your time learning HTML code?

First, the space management: again, look around your room. What does it look like? Do you have hanging files so that you can find your papers? This includes all of your ideas for articles, blogs, and notes from classes you have taken as well as important financial and corporation papers. It includes business cards from potential partners you have met and notes to yourself on subjects with which you should be following up.

What kind of business calendar do you have? Is it accessible? One marketing coach I had actually handed out a big yearly scheduling calendar and sticky notepads for all attendees. She said that is how she got started in her seven-figure business, and she stated that she still uses them regularly to roll out her launches for the year. She is a seven-figure- plus marketing guru! These things work because they are simple and elegant and you don't have to learn obscure spread-sheet details. You can just plot it out on paper, and use the template for your daily action steps.

But, if you have misplaced a month's worth of notes under a pile of papers from year ago, you are probably in trouble, at least in the short run. You will have to get a handle on your lack of organization so that your brilliant mind can start to function again!

I have a friend whose house is so cluttered that she claims she can't begin to do anything toward starting a new business or even a hobby because every time she comes home, she gets totally distraught by her inability to turn around let alone do anything productive. Clearly, the first baby step for her is to take that first piece of paper off the big pile, blow off the dust, and decide where a better place for it might be. If her first year in business is merely doing that, she would be doing herself a service: no judgment, no berating herself, just taking the action step that is right in front of her.

I do not say this casually nor do I think it is easy to begin with a huge project like that. Sometimes the necessity of having to move is the motivation to begin a general cleaning event, but if you are not forced by external necessity, the creation of an internal commitment is important. I still marvel at how happy and clear I feel when I do a minor cleaning out of my "stuff."

Things hold energy. We are affected by the energy of objects that no longer matter to us, yet we keep them nearby out of habit. It takes courage to give away or throw away things that once had meaning for us. Yet when we do let go of them, there is room for new ideas and objects that are more appropriate for our current situations.

One story I have to illustrate the idea that things hold energy concerns the time I was working in a stress management clinic as an energy healer. I would be finishing the session, having assisted an opening and release of symptoms with my clients. As they were sitting up from the table, the first thing they would see were psychology books with such titles as <u>Schizophrenia in the Teenage Patient</u> or <u>The Abusive Relationship</u>. Finally, I realized that it probably wasn't such a good idea to have those books in the room at all. What a pleasure it was to eventually replace them with my healing books!

Feng Shui is the Chinese art of spatial flow. The Chinese understood that there is an energy flow in people's bodies as well as in their environment, and so creating a pleasing environment is a worthy endeavor that brings peace and harmony to the home and to the person living there. I would take it one step further and add that it also creates a fertile environment in which to create new ideas and manifest one's dreams, and—if these issues are not addressed—there is a disconnection from the proper fulfillment of the idea.

I don't have the "pack-rat" tendency myself—someone who keeps everything she has ever bought—but I feel empathy for those who are. Yet, I also believe that the unwillingness to let go of old things, old memories, and reminders of times long gone is a sure way to stay stuck in life. The unwillingness to see that hoarding for what it is—a fear of the future and inability to let go of the past—will be a huge detriment to your well being.

The best thing I ever did for myself in the management of my own space was to buy a basic book on Feng Shui. Because this art teaches you how to create flow in your environment, you are actively bringing balance and beauty into your home. Flow includes color and proportion and the placing of objects carefully in certain configurations to either increase a quality you want to enhance (prosperity, for example) or decrease constricted quality (stagnation, procrastination). The practice achieves more balance and harmony within the home, using the natural elements of earth, water, fire, air, and metal as the metaphors for gently bringing your life into balance and harmony.

Using crystals in the home for a similar purpose offers energetic physical avenues for creating simplicity, clarity, harmony, and peace. I use crystals for energy healing, but I have loved them and used them in many ways to amplify energy, calm overactive electromagnetic currents, and balance my own energy. They can also be used for meditation and healing. Feng Shui and working with crystals are two specialty practices that I encourage you to learn. Let your intuition lead you to finding the appropriate teachers or books for study.

The most valuable thing you can do for the management of your environment is to become aware of the negative effect that clutter has for your business and life. There are whole businesses created to help people manage their clutter. I believe that coaching is an important aid for business owners to shift old patterns around clutter so they can learn to run their home-based business with ease.

If you start to become aware of the "energy" around your stuff, you will—at the very least—know how harmful it is to ignore this important element for success in your life, and you will have new options for taking care of the problem.

The daily practices of energy management, and the choices you make concerning your space, can be treated like a dance. You are choosing consciously every day how you want your day to go. It is a spiritual practice—focusing on the importance of beauty—that comes from making more considered and conscious choices about what you will buy and what you will bring into your home. It is also concerned with having the discipline to choose what you don't want. And it is a dance with that which you will let go. I have given away many beautiful things because the energy of the object had completed its purpose for me, and there was often someone whom I thought would

benefit from having it. This is ongoing work, a true practice at which you will sometimes be very successful and sometimes not, but treat it as holy work, and bring your love and compassion to it.

It is about listening to the clear voice within that helps to be aware of whether the object is holding "dead" energy or "live" energy. This is the same way we tend to the care of our gardens and our animals. Everything is alive, and we are either tending with thoughtfulness or forgetting with thoughtlessness. In the end, we are creating the lives that our consciousness is directed toward. We have unlimited resources through our own minds and hearts to create the life of our dreams or the life of our discontent. Our outer environment shows a lot about who we are. There is a direct connection between our awareness of our environment and our productivity and success. It has a huge effect on our day-to-day happiness and peacefulness as well.

Now for time management:

Does your day get away from you? Do you have a schedule that you keep? Do you generally go to bed and get up at the same time every day? Do you get enough sleep? When you awaken, do you have a ritual that you do every day that is sacred to you, or are you thrown into the first crisis that presents? What throws you off your balance? We tend to get emotionally triggered by the first external project of the day and then lose focus for the things that would have otherwise been tended to.

Stephen R. Covey wrote a bestseller book—<u>The Seven Habits of Highly Effective People</u> (Simon and Schuster New York, 1989)—in which he tells a story of going to the school that his son attended and giving a talk to the children. He first placed six rocks into a jar and asked the children if the jar was filled up. They all agreed that it was indeed filled. Then he placed pebbles into the jar, which filled the space between the rocks, and he again asked the children whether the jar was filled. They again agreed. He then proceeded to place sand in the jar and it filled the space between the pebbles. He once again asked the children if the jar was now filled, and they again agreed, at which time he also agreed. He said to them "If you don't start with your six rocks, the jar will soon fill up with the smaller things, and you will not be able to accomplish the important activities of your day."

I love this story. I tell it to all of my coaching clients because it is such a great analogy for how time can get

swallowed up in a day and how we inadvertently lose our ability to accomplish the things we really want to accomplish. So we must honor our six rocks early in the day, and ascertain what they are. I encourage my clients to take time—even a few minutes first thing in the morning—to decide what those six rocks are.

One might be doing yoga practice or taking a walk in nature. Another could be to make that dreaded revenue-generating call first thing before email or other people's needs take you off course. That way, at the end of the day, you know that you have accomplished the most important things and let the rest fill in like sand between the rocks. Otherwise it is only sand all day long.

I was taught by my coaches that moving through something that feels uncomfortable is the only way to break through a pattern of procrastination. Often, procrastination feels like confusion and overwhelm, but it is only because we make up logical reasons to obscure the facts from ourselves. We often make poor choices about what we need to accomplish. Then we let the day get out of control by making more choices that are the logical outgrowth of what we put in place initially that are not in the interest of our goals.

This is called the "shiny-object syndrome": the wrong approach to your business. Your reasoning for listening to a lecture instead of doing your work often seems sound because you know you can grow through learning more about what someone has to say about some aspect of business of which you are not clear, but the subconscious reason for engaging in the activity is because you feel that you don't quite know enough yet and are listening to another business owner share her information with you instead of your creating your own information.

This is a time-management problem. A whole lifetime can go by without accomplishing much. The world needs your voice. Your clients are waiting for you to show up so they can grow; your particular way of teaching is unlike anyone else's. I believe that the way you can help people is divinely appointed to come from your lips and your voice and your wisdom. It acts more like a transmission than words or scripts on a page.

It is you coming fully present to the work that you are meant to do directly from your heart's desire. If it didn't, you would not be attracted to learning this material. You would be doing something else. This is what I call your "soul connection." It comes through you as you bring your soul presence into the world through your teachings. Your soul can be found by looking deeply into your own eyes. All that you are and all that you want to express is easily revealed to you as you take off the masks you have gathered over years of trying to comply with an idea of who or what you should be only to lose the connection and life energy of your true life's work.

As you cover over the wisdom of your own message and truth, you lose much more than the immediate opportunity. Your intuition dims, and you shut down the passion with which you exuberantly began to manifest your dreams.

Once you have lost connection, some of your innocence goes with it, and it will be much harder to bring it back. Of course, it is never gone exactly, but, rather, it becomes vague and murky. Bringing your soul energy back to your center is spiritual work. It requires you to pay attention to how your energy moves and to invite the alignment of your higher Self with Source/Spirit so that your soul presence can reveal itself to you.

It is as though your soul presence has to come down from somewhere else, from the Heavens and from the Earth simultaneously, where you are aligned and connected as the meeting place of both, which then extends and expands through you as you. Yes, you hold this much power!

The result is a huge amount of peace and calm and courage to speak from your wise center. It fills you and guides you. By connecting consciously with this energy and awareness, you recognize that you are on a soul's journey, and all the experiences you are having in this Earth experience are enhancing your life.

Then, when you depart this world, you take this essence with you as a deep knowing of the soul-self, and the next time you can come back with all your accomplishments as well as the karma from the previous incarnations to refine and clarify the next time around.

I believe that many people think this is magical thinking because there is so little recall of our past incarnations. But healers and shamans see the aspect of the incarnation of the soul as normal and evident. Healers don't usually have to learn about this truth about us; they know it instinctively.

I tell my clients who do not understand about the transmigration of their own souls to see it as a metaphor or "just so" story about what is possible and not to take the idea too literally. This seems to assuage their skepticism somewhat, but I have learned to accept their skepticism because, otherwise, I cannot do the energetic healing and clearing that is so necessary.

I do remember a number of my previous incarnations, and it is fun to have that all information, yet this present life is the important life we live, and what we do with what we are given is what really matters. My philosophy is one that centers on self-forgiveness, clearing (healing), and completion of our karmic ties. Living fully and letting the past be in the past with gentleness and forgiveness allows us to do what we are meant to do and be in this lifetime.

Then, all the people we encounter can be honored, and the experiences we have can be more fully appreciated.

I am a spiritual teacher and energy healer. Doing this work is my purpose and what I have come here to do. When I divert my attention from this focus, I am less happy. I also have my life lessons, which seem to be concerned with issues of powerlessness, so I have to be ever- vigilant when my ego misinterprets events, and I play out a victim mentality. When I can instead use the opportunity to take my own power, give myself permission to choose my interpretations of events, and not give my power away, I am in my purpose. Taking control in this way has proved that it is useful to take objective inventory of my emotional life and allow the truer, more improved me to emerge.

Other people have entirely different obstacles to overcome, so I must have patience with things I don't know and show compassion and understanding for these obstacles. We often encounter this with our intimate friends and lovers, which leads to a greater possibility for drama and intrigue, yet also a greater possibility for true patience and assistance. Other people often hold up the mirror for us to look at aspects of ourselves not readily known to us or comfortable to confront.

So what does this all have to do with managing our time? Everything. Nobody else can help us feel safe in our bodies or help us feel comfortable or on purpose. Our time is our biggest asset, and we have license to do with it as we may. There are only 24 hours in a day for all of us. Time is a factor that cannot be extended. When the day is done, it is done. How we think and how we spend our time is up to us. Why, then, would we spend any time at all chastising ourselves or letting someone else dictate how we should use our time?

Nobody has the authority to diminish you or enslave you. Some of us are so emotionally abused by others that even when the person is not around, we and create negative outcomes for ourselves. We become victims of the mind, of thoughts and feelings that, had we contemplated them more carefully, we would realize that these ideas are faulty and not even ours.

You can turn your life around, get out of debt, and create a successful business relatively quickly if you follow the appropriate actions. If you can do the necessary inner work to be more mindful about what is possible, managing your time and the things you do with it will lead you out of fear, procrastination, self-doubt, and frustration.

It is up to you and nobody else. Your future is in your hands alone. All you need to do is to take responsibility now for all of it. Ask where you have allowed someone else to be responsible for your behavior, where you have abdicated your own power of decision and choice, and where you have allowed yourself to be a victim of someone else's demands of you.

As you take your time and power back and start making choices that support your dreams, you will be amazed at

what you can accomplish. Let go of all that does not serve you: the ideas of lack; the excuses that have you thinking you don't know enough or have the time, money, or the smarts to accomplish your dream. Instead, listen for the opportunities that are already around you that could be taking you on a direct path toward realizing your vision: not tomorrow, now. Now.

And finally I want to speak about simplifying:

What have you been hanging onto for too long that you don't really need anymore? Old letters from an old flame? Doing a daily practice out of habit that no longer has meaning for you? Doing something for a family member because they expect it of you, not because your heart is in it?

Simplifying sometimes comes in the form of creating better boundaries in relationships. What or whom are you spending too much time helping when you could be giving that time to yourself? Are you in a relationship with someone who continuously interrupts you when you are doing something creative or productive because they think your life doesn't matter as much as theirs? If this is the case, slowly and gently set a boundary that starts to let them know that your work is as important as theirs.

Granted, we live in families, and every person has a job to do. If your husband earns most of the family's money, you might feel obligated to do more of the housework and childcare. You may even love it; however, if you can't get out from under when you have a dream of starting your own business—and ultimately fulfilling more of a monetary partnership with your husband—how are you going to be able to turn things around? How will you come to have more balance of chores and power within the family?

Or perhaps you are in a job that you don't like and dream of working for yourself. However, you need the income and can't think of how you could possibly make the switch to working for yourself, so you stay in the job you hate and slowly lose sight of your yearnings.

There is grace is simplifying. Figure out what the minimum is that you actually need so that you can start methodically shifting out of the life you are living and into one that is aligned with what you envision.

Each circumstance is different, so coaching in this area has to be customized for your particular situation. However, the first thing you can do is simplify and decide what you actually need now while making the transition to what you want.

You may need to stay in the job you have for now, but you can still decide get up earlier each morning and start putting in place the coaching or healing practice about which you have dreamed. You can get training and finance your next step while staying in the job you have. Think about what you can give up: perhaps the designer clothes that have gone with the corporate position you have held, the dinners out, the magazine subscriptions,

all the extras you have become accustomed to. Simplifying is looking at your money flow and deciding whether getting out of debt is more important than living the old lifestyle. As you implement a debt- payoff plan that puts you in control and gets you focused and moving toward important goals, you will begin to feel more empowered and focused.

This one change can empower you to take more command of your future. You are reaching for new goals and getting the education, the coaching, and the mindset you need to break out of the rut that has held you back. Your time and your money become aligned with what you are saying that you want, and moving in this new direction helps to build the kind of momentum that will carry you to your new vision. You are creating your future and not just dreaming about it.

I believe in the power of simplifying. In clearing clutter, you are making a conscious decision about what you want and making it happen one step at a time. You are letting go of non-essentials. Old, unused items in your home hold energy. Habitual thoughts hold the energy of stagnation. Even your attitudes and beliefs about money hold energy that is either fluid or stagnant. Money is energy in motion. As you let go of what is no longer serving your highest purpose, new ideas and creativity are often the reward.

For example, have you ever thought of the excess weight you may carry on your body as the emotional baggage that you have not been willing to deal with? I have found with my clients that weight gain is more an emotional than a physical issue. Your feelings about the past, people for whom you still hold anger or sadness all count toward withholding that manifests as excess weight. As you clear and release the hold these situations have upon you, new and more vital energy can take their place. New ideas come to you to fill the void. New projects come to mind. New people show up for you! And one day you may even notice that those stubborn extra pounds you have been carrying are also gone.

You are in command of your creations because you are saying no to what you no longer need in order to get more of what you want. You are becoming your own best friend and listening to what your heart and your intuition are telling you to do. You are giving yourself permission to do and feel and act from your truth. You defy others' expectations of you. You are actually following through on your intuitive voices that can direct you on the path of your highest and best goals. And it feels good because you are making your self-care a priority. This includes listening to your inner muse: your personal guidance that has always been available.

You are being guided by your own inner knowing as to how to progress. You get a "hit," you go with it, and something good happens; you meet the right person at the right time that takes you even more in the direction you want to move. You feel excited and on purpose and in sync with people and events, so you start to take even more chances.

Most of all, you feel empowered. You take over leadership of your own life. You continue to let go of what no longer serves you and are willing to change direction if needed. You start to have an energy about you that is magnetic and energized, and subsequently you have even more courage to listen to what is coming to you through your inner guidance. You trust your heart and your gut. You let go again and the cycle continues. It feels good and you are on fire!

There is no other process than this. This is the process of spiritualizing your business. You are simply bringing yourself into alignment and allowing your dreams to unfold before your very eyes. It lets you be both visible and unstoppable. You are not second guessing your choices or worrying about what others might think about you or about your business. Your vision is clear, and there are fewer and fewer obstacles in your way. You see the positive effect of more money coming in; you know how to speak clearly and directly from your heart; and all the while you are living your dreams that emanate from your essential, divine nature.

This is, of course, the way it is meant to be because the Universe is abundant. Look around you. There is no scarcity out there except when and if you stop believing in yourself. You belong just as much as anyone else, and you demonstrate this truth by taking your place as a leader and trusting the outcome. Being seen and heard by others comes from being willing and able to speak up, share your wisdom, and then ask for the business. This is the essence of the sacred selling process that I teach all of my clients to use for their sales. It works because it is very natural and aligned with their most heartfelt desires to serve others and thereby to create a better world for all.

It includes self-fulfillment through offering meaningful service, a great lifestyle, and it brings more light to the world.

The new opportunities are then used as scaffolding to create even stronger structures for your offerings. You use the money that you are generating to make even better offerings, receive more support, and increase your business to its full flourishing. And you are fulfilling the number one universal law: More Life for All.

Also called the Law of Increase, this law states that life is always wanting to unfold. If you have ever planted a garden of flowers or vegetables and forgotten to water them at the critical times in the heat of the summer, you have probably experienced this law in its negative form. However, as soon as you change your behavior and start watering again, you will see the most amazing example of the Law of Increase in effect. The flowers bloom from their withered state, the tomatoes ripen on the vine, and all is well.

All you have to do is wait for spring to see the Law of Increase in full flourishing! The buds are on the trees, then the leaves, then the full shade of the summer. Inevitably the millions of leaves will fall to the ground in autumn and the quiet of winter, only to be restored once again to the budding in spring.

This is the way it is meant to be. All you have to do is act in sync with this abundance, and things will fall into place for you. Look around, and act upon the opportunities that come your way, even if they don't look like opportunities at the time. Try to notice whether your objections to moving forward with your ideas come from a place of scarcity and lack: for example, that you can't afford to pay for your venture or that you don't know where you will find the time to do the necessary work. When you are aligned with your vision, the work doesn't feel hard. You ride on the energy of your enthusiasm and vision. You are on your path and on your way!

Chapter Five: Claim Your Vision, Know Your Worth

Your vision is your deep soul connection revealed to you. In my mind, the words "vision" and "soul" are interchangeable. Vision connection is soul connection. Do you have a clear vision of what you want? Are you connected with it consciously and consistently even when things don't look so good? Do you know why you are not yet achieving your goals? What do you think might be the biggest obstacle to achieving them? Can you articulate your vision clearly and declare it with conviction?

Are you willing to do the inner work you must do in order to clear the obstacles to manifesting your true vision and soul's work? Most of us are our own worst enemies when it comes to mastering our potential because we can't see what we are doing to obscure the path. Our blind spots tend to get the best of us. We are often self-sabotaging without even knowing it!

So Key Number 5 is knowing your own worth. Going deep within and finding out why you are blocking the manifestation will turn everything around for you. But it takes a huge commitment and investment of time and courage to look so deeply within. Your ego mind will not want you to travel there. Remember, we are hard-wired in our brains not to take chances. Yet it is often small shifts in your mindset that make all the difference.

This includes letting go and moving beyond old beliefs long held about money and success, which must be addressed and cleared. It often includes an inventory of habitual patterns and addictions that must be understood and released. So asking your soul to reveal your life purpose vision may be the very most important question of all.

Then you can ask, "Where do I want to go?" This question puts you in the director's chair of your own life, so you become the leader instead of the follower of someone you have deemed more knowledgeable than yourself. It is only when you take leadership of your own affairs that you get any traction. Then beyond that you must stand for your business and ask for people to buy from you. Otherwise you don't have a business.

The SHINE Factor:

Are you ready to step up and SHINE? When you are living from the integral state of yourself, where you are not imitating anyone else and where you are not creating your life from a template of another's design, you are getting closer. As you begin to touch the zone of your own genius you are coming even closer to the energetic center of your glowing. The SHINE factor comes out of making a connection with your most brilliant vision on the soul level and then moving through any energetic clutter or energy drains you might have that keep you in hiding and not shouting it out from the rooftops.

Have you been afraid to be seen, really seen? Has your voice been left mute because you have been afraid of what other people might think if you speak from your heart and mind? Are you afraid to make a mistake? Do you pull your tongue back into your throat because you don't want to be heard too much? You are not alone in this.

It is said that public speaking is the number-one most feared activity. Have you heard the joke that most people would rather be in the casket rather than having to be the one giving the eulogy at someone's funeral? I still laugh when I hear that joke. What about all of the "best men" at weddings blowing their speeches or the pianist forgetting the beginning of the sonata when they go out on stage to play?

The extreme fear of being seen and heard—otherwise known as stage fright—is a hurdle that you must overcome if you want to thrive in your business. There is no other way. Even being the CEO of a small business requires you to be able to speak clearly and with authority to those who might be your prospective clients.

You also need to be able to claim your authority with your team. You hired them to help you increase your business, but what if you were so wishy-washy that you never created clear project parameters for them or didn't have the will to complain if you were unhappy with their performance?

You cannot leave people guessing, or they will not able to produce for you. Corporations spend massive amounts of money uplifting the emotional lives of their employees and helping to improve inter-office communications so their businesses run optimally. Happiness on the job has a cost benefit to a corporation's bottom line.

It is the same for the small business. If you have not mastered the ability to share your intentions as well as offer suggestions for the realization of your goals with your employees, you will be wasting valuable time and money without much to show for your efforts. Going down this road will leave you wondering why your business failed or never took off in the first place. So learn to speak up in the most authentic way possible.

I struggled with stage fright all my life. I hated standing in front of other people and speaking. Even the seemingly innocuous act of going around a circle stating names filled me with jitters. It's true. Simply stating my name was enough for trepidation. I must have thought that people were going to judge me, so the emotion was a fear of rejection or not fitting in. If this is you too, there might be a bit of a learning curve here for you.

I encourage you to get a handle on this now if you have any concern about your public persona because it will have an impact on how other people react to you. It can make the difference between someone saying yes to working with you or passing you by. Because I have done the work to overcome my own fear of presenting myself, this topic has become my expertise. I had to work through my own stage fright and have spent years studying people who have natural charisma. I have learned the bottom-line costs of how personal discomfort has an impact on the impressions you make; I am equipped to take you to the other side of your discomfort! I know you can benefit from the mistakes I have made and learn from the difficulties I have surmounted. Please reach out for help if you need it. The amount of movement toward your goals from this kind of specific help will astound you and move your business to the next level. Here is where the adage "when you fail to plan, you plan to fail" holds a painful truth in the bottom line of your business. Getting clarity as well as skill in being more magnetic will bring benefits you never thought existed.

The single best marketing tool you will ever have is your sparkling presence in front of your ideal clients. You could have them eating out of your hand or tuning out completely, depending upon your skill in reaching out to them. As you create your specialized signature talk, representing your knowledge and expertise, and do not skip over the body/mind educational work necessary to refine your presentation, you will see an exponential shift in your success.

Selling is a very delicate process. As you offer more of your true self to the conversation, people will be drawn to working with you and may not even know why. You just have something they like and want for themselves. Essentially, they want to be like you. The connection you are making is nothing more than this, but you have to have worked through all of the things that make you not want to reveal your vulnerability and opinions. Your courage has to be authentic and from the heart.

If, however, you are reticent to speak to someone at a networking meeting or you become tongue-tied and embarrassed when you have to share what it is that you do in front of your audience, this will have a negative impact on your success. This will also have a negative impact on your bottom line; you will wonder why people are not saying yes to your offers.

And what if you cannot even muster enough courage to ask for the sale? If you cannot get to the point of having the important conversation of asking for the business, your ideal client will walk away, and you will see your business tank.

I cannot tell you how many times I have spoken with heart-centered healers, coaches, and entrepreneurs who have told me they hate marketing. They say they love their craft and wish that they could just do their work and have people somehow magically knock on their doors.

Frankly, I have felt that way too, but that attitude makes for a wonderful hobby and not a business. You may feel very pleased with your work and your ability to facilitate healing for others, yet you will lose out on your true talents and gifts for changing lives and participating in the healing of the planet that is so much needed at this time. Work will trickle in, and you will see a smattering of livelihood but no real impact.

The good news is that there is an art to all of this. It takes some honest soul searching and some clear insight into your habits and behaviors, with a willingness to change things that need to be shifted, but it is easier than

you think to step through this hurdle. The reward is great when you put in the effort.

There are many people who have no problem speaking publicly. We marvel at them because they seem to have nerves of steel, and owning the stage looks natural for them. If you are not one of those who speak well naturally, you could be experiencing discomfort just thinking about presenting yourself publicly. I have found that there are three important keys to help you move through the discomfort of being seen and heard.

Key Number 1: Before you talk about your work, connect with your big vision. This includes two things: your passionate vision and who you know yourself to be deep down in your soul. It includes an intuitive knowing of what you came here to do. It may be to serve others through a particular talent or skill you have. It could be that you are a builder, an artist. It is what is already singing in your soul. You may be really good at inspiring others to act in service toward their goals, and so coaching is the thing to do for your business. You may be a mother, and your desire is to have children and give of your talents of encouragement and compassion. You could be burning to create a dance company or an orphanage.

If you can commit to aligning yourself with your inner truth in the work you are doing—the work that is yours alone to do as your contribution to the healing of the world—you can get some leverage for pushing through the worry about how it is going to happen.

This is the work you would be doing even if there were absolutely no monetary gain as a result of doing it. This is work that comes out of the depths of your being and gives you a sense of purpose and aliveness. It turns you on and makes you happy to do it. It is you following the thread of your passions. It is you claiming your vision.

For this reason, we call it your big "why." Why do you feel so passionate about saving animals from mistreatment? Why does your heart break when you think about poverty, illiteracy, women being bullied? How much do you love coaching little league? Have you always wanted to be a doctor when you grew up? Your big "why" is already at your finger tips. It is your life purpose that reveals itself to you as you ask the question.

If you can really connect with your big vision, you are on your way to the manifestation and the expression of it because you could march right up on stage and talk about it from your heart for hours. This is key. Your soul-inspired work is work that you love to do, and it is work that needs to be done by you. I will say that again. It is work that needs to done to heal the world, and it needs to be done by you and nobody else.

This characteristic about you is the only connection you need for monetizing your gifts and talents. The people with whom you are meant to work will find you because you are speaking directly to their soul. They may have heard the exact same words from someone else, but the way you say it makes the difference for them. They start to perk up and listen to you because you are reaching their hearts. They start to feel drawn to you as an answer to their inner prayers. It is a matter of vibration and magnetic connection. There is a comingling of energies between you and them. One coach of mine used to say "they are already on their way to you."

You have connected to your ideal client in this way. The others listening to you may not be able to hear your words or be inspired because the way they need to learn simply requires a different approach. Not to worry; they are not meant to work with you and will find help from someone else. You are attracting the people who have problems that you can solve and will hear the message you are sharing. They will have a direct connection to you and want to receive help from you.

There is more than enough wisdom to go around for all of us, and, in this abundant Universe, we are all meant to serve and be served. There need be no competition or suspicion, just readiness at the right and perfect time to bring the manifestation forward into the physical realm out from your ideas and dreams.

In fact, our world is ready for quite a new way of doing business in general. In a World Summit in 2009, the Dalai Lama was quoted as saying "The future of the world belongs to the Western Woman." I think what he meant by this is that there is room for women doing business in a feminine way. Women don't have to turn into men in order to have clients. There is room in the marketplace for a return of a softer and more feminine way. No competition.

Women are having greater impact on their communities and a more powerful worldly presence by staying within what they do naturally: creating cooperative ventures and being true to their natural tendencies to share in communities. The old model still works, but women don't have to be little men in order to deliver the wealth of

knowledge they wish to share. It is a model that needs to be practiced. Women-for- women communities are springing up all over. Niche markets are forming outside of the corporate model, where women can support each other, buy from each other, be clients of each other.

I have seen women entrepreneurs excel greatly in the past decade, some creating six- and seven-figure spiritually based businesses in less than three years! There is no reason to believe this cannot happen for you as well.

With the correct approach, the correct mindset, and the correct business model, your business could easily blossom. This model would serve you gracefully where you could dance in the flow of your opportunities and help nurture others' growth and wellbeing, where you can step up and shine wherever you are and have huge impact on people's lives.

Key Number 2 for building your soul-inspired business for greater impact is to truly know your value. We tend to "compare and despair" when we first put our work out for others to see. We keep our prices down. We wait and watch for how other people are promoting their businesses, and borrow from them; we even use the same language as others who have proven themselves successful in the marketplace.

But if you align with your own sense of worth, you need not imitate others. There will be a great outpouring of creativity directly through you. You act as a channel and conduit for the right message that needs to be expressed to the right people. You do this on faith and without censorship because you are in the flow of your good work. You trust your vision and act upon it, and you find and appreciate support from those who can assist you as you act on faith.

The safety net will appear as you jump. Things will come to you: ideas, inventions, ways of marketing and connecting with your people that you had not considered. Being on the front edge of what's next is the way to go. And the only way to do that is to have real quiet time to go within and listen to the inner guidance that you find as you take the time to listen. This is your intuition in action. You have an idea, and you run with it. You get a "hit" that you should travel to a particular event or work with a particular coach, and things magically open up for you.

The right person shows up with the answer to a question you have been pondering.

There is a reason for this: You are moving into your flow in faith that there are others through which the energy of creativity pours. You know your value, and you don't second-guess it by thinking you don't yet know enough or you don't have the right wardrobe or hair. You don't obsess about your weight or other self-critical thoughts. All these distractions and complicating factors fall away, and you grow in courage to just get out and start sharing because you know your worth, and you are not concerning yourself with being perfect before you roll out your offerings.

One of my coaches used to say you have to "build the plane while you fly it." Airplanes spend 97% of their airtime course-correcting to reach their destination. Imagine that you have the amount of faith necessary to just start flying the plane and feel comfortable with the knowledge that you will most likely have to course-correct along the way. What kind of abandon would you feel? It's fun!

On the other hand, what if you said something that made you embarrassed or you didn't have your facts 100%

correct? Could you live through the shame? Probably. It is so much more important to take imperfect action than to take no action. How else could you possibly get the experience without just getting up there and trying?

But if your feelings of worthiness need some work, there will be fear until you get some success. Until you see that the imperfect action is actually fun and that your mistakes didn't matter so much, your heart will pound. Maybe you are afraid you are going to forget what you planned to say or you get light-headed right before you go on stage. Maybe you do forget what you were going to say and you mess up the first few minutes of the talk. It is just part of it. Ask any public speaker about their most embarrassing engagements, and they will probably have a whole list for you. But if you know—in the depth of your heart—that you are worthy, that you have value just because you are a human being in a community and that your voice counts, then you are more likely to take the risk and show up and share.

And the end result is so worth it. This is because we do live in community, and it is only in sharing and in connecting with others that we can even participate at all.

Then you benefit in the experience of all that human warmth and responsiveness coming your way. You are energized and fed by the energy. You grow and shift according to the responses you get, and you practice. That's all. You just have to get out and practice and course- correct as needed.

I will say it now: You are worthy, you are beautiful, and your voice counts. You don't need my permission for that to be true; it is true because you are a child of the Infinite Intelligence of the Universe and the world needs you to show up authentically, vulnerably, and completely as yourself.

You were never meant to be anyone other than who you already are. By taking the risk to get out and take action toward speaking and being visible, other people will have the opportunity to learn from you. What if there were someone whose life you would change if you could muster the courage to become more visible? If you stay in hiding, that person will never find you, and that would be a shame.

Knowing your worth goes a long way toward being your authentic, vulnerable self and creating a vehicle for your best and most vital expression. It will also take the form of your most natural expression. I have a colleague who

crochets amazing hearts and shawls for people while she talks with them. That activity is unique to her and is her natural creativity and expression.

I am bringing her up at this moment as an example of doing what you love and trusting that good things will come to you. In one instance, I was talking for an hour or so with this friend while she crocheted and when we were finished she gave me a beautiful red crocheted heart, which rests on my altar to this day. I felt that she was dancing in the flow of her excellence in the most natural and nurturing way, and she had a beautiful piece of art to give at the end of our conversation. It was a gift from her soul; she didn't have to try to do anything. She felt comfortable and peaceful within herself, and something unique and positive emerged from her creativity.

For you, it could be a dance, a poem, or even just a smile offered at the perfect moment. It could come through the volunteer work you do at an animal shelter or your church or synagogue. It could take the form of really listening to friends in pain and giving them a sense of hope for the future at a time when they really needed it.

Each time we connect with who we are in our most authentic selves, we set something in motion that will continue creating into the future. As you define and refine your own inner strength and wellness,—that with which nobody has to approve or agree—you are moving toward your dream.

Your sense of worth and value are your biggest assets. Knowing your worth takes your offering to the next level of mastery. You can more and more influence others with your gifts and talents. It is simply a matter of creating a container for your visibility.

Key Number 3: Be willing to step up and step out and really SHINE your light. Once you have created the container for your big vision, and you have firmly established the truth of your worthiness, there is merely ther small matter of marketing in such a way that you allow for the biggest splash possible. Why not? Life is waiting.

Remember Billy Crystal in the Saturday Night Live skit saying: "It is better to look marvelous than to feel marvelous"? Well, you get to have both. You look marvelous because your inner light is shining. You are a bright magnetic presence with the capacity to own the stage.

What would it take to really feel marvelous? Imagine what you would be wearing, how you would walk on stage, how you would feel in your body. If it is anything but relaxed and excited, you will want to pay close attention to what I am going to share with you right now.

I have made a career out of helping people feel more comfortable in their own bodies. My tag line for my Alexander Technique business is "being well in your own body." Another favorite quote is: "If you wear out your body, where will you live?" Listen to your body because it is telling you how safe you are. If you feel really safe and happy, you will be in a position where nobody can throw you off your game, even if you have just stepped out in front of a thousand people.

Of course, you will want to have done your homework to be prepared for your talk and have a well-crafted speech. The words and ideas you share must be organized and consistent with who you are, but this first piece about overcoming stage fright is important. We can never separate our physical presence from our emotional well-being. We are one unified psychophysical whole. If you feel scared, acknowledge it. If you feel as if your nerves are going to make you faint or throw up, let that exist, too;

don't push it away. Most likely, the wave of nausea will pass.

The key is to not let it overpower you or have an interpreted meaning attached to it. It is that little negative voice that sneaks in with interpretation that I call your "gremlins." You have to tame them.

One of the things I still say to myself right before I have to go on stage is: "Wow, you are really nervous right now, Diane." I acknowledge it. But then I visualize a process that opens my energy down into the floor and up and out through the top of my head into the room so that I see the room and all the people in it, filling with light. And I make the decision that I am a vessel for light and that I am able to channel that light so that my voice can remain calm and my countenance peaceful. I, in effect, choose to be calm. It is an order to self.

It really works. This is a basic spiritual healing practice that I learned long ago. Whenever I do this practice I calm down and get grounded.

Energetically, we fly out the top of our heads when we are nervous. We have to come back in! This has happened to me often when I have had to perform dance or to speak, yet I always receive the response from my audiences afterward that I looked calm and confident. No exceptions. Even though my palms were sweaty and my heart was beating, I appeared centered and confident.

As your speech begins, you may feel all of these things, but, as you are also making eye contact with the audience and receiving their energetic responses, a feedback loop begins, and you start to settle in to your talk. Just remember to stay on topic and be vulnerable and truthful, and you will shine. People will love to hear your story, and they will listen with rapt attention if you are authentic.

Also, there is a prep time for going on stage that is all about the time itself. You usually know when it is a few moments before you have to go on stage. This is the time to breathe and do whatever visualization techniques that work for you. You may be pleasantly surprised how well things go when you can come into sync with time.

Take your time and breathe. We forget to breathe when we feel nervous. So breathe and remember that you have time to get your point across. Have you ever seen children perfoming? They tend to speak faster and faster because their internal clock is moving too fast. The same is true for adults, but your adult mind can monitor more effectively than a child can.

What I like to think about is how much time and love and energy I have spent preparing my presentation and how valuable and important it is for me to share what I have. You can give yourself a little pep talk. Then finally there is a little trick you can use right before you go on stage.
You can tell yourself "this will all be over in an hour." Silly I know, but if you project into the future when you are already finished you can come backwards in time to make it even better because it hasn't started yet. In this way, you are compressing time and making it work for you instead of against you.

Here is my story about stage fright: Perhaps it was because I was always moving to new schools in the middle of the year when I was young (my father was a pilot for the Air Force, and we moved frequently) but I went to twelve schools in twelve years and always felt like the new girl in class. All I wanted to do was shrink away from the attention. Even saying my name unnerved me! That first visibility was torture for me. I just wanted to hide from the exposure. Everyone else knew one another, but I was on display, or so I thought.

I have pictures of myself at seven or eight years old where my shoulders were curved forward and I was looking out like I would die if someone took my picture or looked at me. What kind of poor helpless thing I was! I was naturally full of life and movement and fun, but those first "being seen" moments were torture for me.

Move on to when I first experienced stage fright playing the piano: Until about ten years old I was fearless on stage. I remember once starting a sonatina at the third movement instead of the first, and I simply kept trying till I figured out what I was doing incorrectly. A woman came up to me and said how brave I was to keep going, and I didn't even know what she was talking about. It made absolutely no difference to me.

Not so a few years later, the fear had settled in, perhaps through the healthy development of the ego, but now playing the piano for other people made my fingers shake and hands go numb. I was scared.

But do take heart, if you can relate to this fear. I once attended a concert of a student of mine who had won the prize soloist position to play a piano concerto at Stony

Brook University, and her hands were shaking the whole time. It made no difference in the beauty of the playing.

She was magnificent. If you cannot contain the fear while performing, you will need to address the issue beforehand so that you can work through it. The audience may not notice your discomfort, so go ahead and fake it! You will eventually enjoy the limelight, I promise.

When I started to choreograph and dance in my own performances in New York, my fear was so intense that my hands and feet would turn blue right before I had to perform. It was as if my body were going haywire. I had to learn to control my nerves, or I would not be able to perform, and all of the passion I had for dance would turn to naught.

If you can relate to anything I have just shared, let me help you reframe the experience for you. Fear is blocked excitement. The way I worked through fear on my own was to channel the fear into excitement and mentally send the energy through my body. Because the mind and the body are unified, you are channeling the mental calm into the physical and feeling the positive results of the connection. People didn't have a clue that my heart was beating and that my palms were sweaty. They usually told me I didn't look nervous at all, which was a big surprise to me.

How I have come to peace with performance is all about the energy. I feel grateful that I did the work to manage my fear. The risk was better than the alternative. The reward is also in the ongoing journey toward more calm, more excitement, and remembering that it is a privilege to share your message with an eager audience.

This now brings me to the last thing I want to share about visibility. What we are sharing has to be of excellent quality. It must have value; hold integrity; have a clearly stated beginning, middle; and end; and needs to be spoken clearly and with enthusiasm. The way to accomplish this is through practicing. Practice so you know your speech thoroughly. Eliminate the parts that feel awkward or inauthentic. This is your baby: your creativity and brilliance in action.

And remember, you really don't have to be perfect. Nobody expects that of you. People want your sincerity and to be able to relate to your story. If you can share yourself in an interesting way, they will love you. Your job is to help them know, like, and trust you. It is your energy they want and your humanity. They want to be moved emotionally by what you say.

You can be fun and joyful and enthusiastic. The word enthusiasm comes from the words in theos or in God. We are God-like beings, and it is our light that we most need to share. To connect our enthusiasm with our God-like nature is to spread more love and more light in the world and do our part.

I believe that it is everyone's mission to bring more light to the world: to do our part in the healing of the world by being a steward in its wellbeing. It is only in connecting to your joy and your truth that you are able to benefit others and succeed in this massive quest of your soul.

Marianne Williamson, the author of "A Return to Love," has the most extraordinary passage from the book that she wrote in 1991 during the height of the AIDS epidemic:

"Our deepest fear is not that we are inadequate. Our deepest fear is that we are powerful beyond measure. It is our light, not our darkness, that most frightens us. We ask ourselves, who am I to be brilliant, gorgeous, talented, fabulous? Actually, who are you not to be? You are a child of God. Your playing small doesn't serve the world.

There's nothing enlightened about shrinking so that other people won't feel insecure around you. We are all meant to shine, as children do. We were born to make manifest the glory of God that is within us. It's not just in some of us; it's in everyone. And as we let our own light shine, we unconsciously give other people permission to do the same. As we're liberated from our own fear, our presence automatically liberates others."

This speaks to the idea of "permission to shine". Nobody gives us that permission; it is already ours for the taking. There is a divinely inspired connection between releasing fear and gaining presence. Your presence is something that only you can offer the world. As you hold Spirit more and more within you, that light will shine brighter and brighter. Children naturally shine unless something has gone wrong for them in their early lives. They also see other people who shine; they naturally gravitate to them and look at them intently. Notice how a little child's attention is riveted to someone who holds a lot of light. I am convinced that they are seeing the bright aura of the person who is attracting their attention. They have not yet filtered the mysterious aspects of the human soul.

You do have permission to shine. You are a child of God; you are innately beautiful and worthy. Whatever illusions you hold about your unworthiness, leave them at the door because they do not serve your highest version of yourself.

A recent quote I came upon was attributed to Lao Tse: "If you are depressed, you are focused on the past; if you have anxiety, you are focused on the future; if you are present and calm, you are in the present." For many people who suffer from depression, this could be a sensitive topic, but I know that the time in my life when I was at my most despairing was after my divorce; I could not let go of the pain and guilt and memories of my past. I was holding on to a vision of the past that was gone. There was no way to get it back, so all I could do was release the self-inflicted guilt and sorrow and go on.

I also know that the three o'clock-in-the-morning anxiety wakefulness that many women feel is completely connected with the anxiety that the future isn't going to go well. You are at a loss of faith when your mind makes that unfortunate choice. If that happens to you, try telling yourself: "I love you, everything's fine, it's not morning yet, go back to sleep," and witness for yourself how such a small act of self-care and kindness can shift your anxiety. It may help you to fall back to sleep blissfully.

Ideally, we could allow ourselves to connect deeply with the delicious immediacy of the now moment and let the past be the past and the future be "not yet." Staying present to ourselves and our environment: the tastes, smells, sounds and sights of what is right in front of us is available and worthy of our attention.

As you become more skillful about paying attention to and deeply listening to those sounds, sights, and people who are right in front of you, you may experience a kind of expansiveness and calm that is wanting when you are in the habitual negative self-talk patterns that are so familiar. It's those gremlins again! Making a shift from needing to speak to wanting to listen is also a way to stay fully present. It lets the vitality of our world keep showing itself to us as refreshing surprises.

I believe we are here to explore, create, and manifest God's glory in the world. It is no big mystery, only the miracle of life. Sometimes, only a small shift in consciousness allows us to be more aware, more alive, present to the moment, and to find happiness and fulfillment in the here and now. Wistfully waiting for the future to present itself could come with a great deal of frustration and disappointment because the present gets lost in the machinations of the intellect in our feeble attempt to force our will upon it.

I grew up with the quote "don't push the river." That message has stayed with me all these years. What happens if we try to push the river?
Not much anyway, so why not instead try to become one with it or, better yet, just enjoy the ride. What is good for you, truly good, may not be nearly what you project outward. The attempt to bend the world to your will could be making you lose the sweetness and the vulnerability of the more subtle rewards that were right in front of you all along.

On the other hand, if you don't go for what you want, the capacity you have for change and creativity could also be lost. There is a balance of all things, a gentle flow that will lead you down your own river. As one coach of mine says, by opening to your flow you get to experience "your little piece of heaven on earth."

Chapter Six: Deepening Your Soul Connection

"The water continually flowed and flowed
But it was always there.
It always stayed the same
And yet every moment it was new."
— Hermann Hesse

Have you ever noticed that your habitual emotional patterns repeat and repeat until you get clarity? Life itself is a journey of increasing consciousness. We are opening through experience to the depths of what it is to be human in all of our vulnerability. It is often our mistakes that bring the biggest lessons. To stay oblivious to your habitual ways of being will sabotage you at every point. And here is the rub: The closer you get to your goal, especially as you start to break through to a new awareness and level of being, the bigger the challenges will show up to throw you off course.

It seems unfair that you put so much time and patience into building your business, start gaining momentum, and begin feeling really good about yourself, when something will happen and weeks go by when you have all but forgotten the progress you made. We need a paradigm shift, but the paradox is that even though it is you who must do all of the inner work, release and change usually comes through the back door as an "aha" and not because of hard work. Instead, it comes out of the blue and from sources you least expected. It often comes not through your own efforts but by taking a break, letting go, walking in nature, getting away from your computer, and out to an event and into the company of others.

This is because people are meant to live in community. You are not meant to be the lone ranger and go it alone. You are meant to receive love and attention and sweetness and connection all along the way. It is in community that our weaknesses are revealed to us and in community where we really grow and change.

It could show up at home through your partner mirroring back to you your tendencies and traits even though you think it is coming from their issues. It could be your coach/mentor/healer showing you a better and more loving way to clear the blocks and imbalances that inevitably resurface, pulling you back to square one. It could even be a traumatic experience or loss that shatters your world and throws you into new, unchartered territory where you have to take a fresh look at yourself and your creations.

This is all meant to wake you up. It might feel as though life has thrown salt on your wound, but the effect often catapults you into a revealed perception of the possible. It will, at the very least, shift your awareness of the ground of your being and push you out of complacency. This is all part of the prescription to move you out of your cozy nest of comfortable misery and into the manifesting of your potential.

Change is good. If you don't change, nothing will happen. Things will go along in the same way that they have been going. You will act the same way and react the same way. You will never have to confront your gremlins because you aren't willing to recognize that they even live inside you. Change is threatening to your ego.

This is a concept so important to understand that I make it a cornerstone of my coaching practice. The ego doesn't want you to change because it perceives change as threatening to your survival. It wants to keep you safe, so any change is to be avoided. You must actively and consciously not listen to the voice of the ego when you want to progress to a new level in your business. Your ego will perceive the risk you are about to take as dangerous, and it will do anything in its power to talk you out of your idea.

On the other side sits the voice of your healing and your intuition, gently whispering to you to go here, go there, seek out that person, take that course, and take that risk. This voice is divinely inspired and gives you ideas and messages from within that make no sense to the ego. It sends you on joy rides and gets you entangled in scary matters of the heart. It expects you to live with no censorship. It doesn't care that you don't know what you are doing. This voice wants you to feel the fear and do it anyway.

So we find ourselves in an internal battle between the voices, and too often we go with the voice trying to keep us safe, small, and not believing in ourselves. Then we miss the opportunities that are right in front of us. We start to rationalize by thinking: "It's too much money; I don't really have the time; I've tried that before, and it didn't work."

Then the pattern sets in on a deeper level, based upon the standard you have set for yourself. The inner critic resets the parameters of creativity and freedom to explore, and you go back to smaller and less dangerous choices. Instead of saying "I'm afraid," you say "It's too big; it costs too much; it's not worth it." But if you were really honest, you would say: "I don't have faith that I can accomplish this," which would at least allow you to stop deceiving yourself.

Most people don't really change much in their lives. If you followed peoples' lives over twenty years, you would likely see them living and acting very much as they always have. Decades evaporate, and with that passing time, dreams also evaporate. We live lives of quiet desperation, not fulfilling the divine promise that resides within us. The promise remains, but it is hidden under a heavy blanket of sadness and lack.

You confuse yourself by starting a creative marketing idea and then abandoning it midway, half forgetting about it, and starting another. Or you make an initial connection with a potential client and forget to follow up. You are not in action toward your goal. It only feels like you are in business because you are busy!

Take a look around your environment and get really still and honest with yourself. Look at the papers on your desk, the emails piling up, and the dust. Become attuned to your surroundings and your breathing. Notice the thoughts that are coming to you. As you become present to your body and to the moment, you will notice the beginnings of a release of tension: physically and psychologically. It is only in this place that you truly have choice for your business. Jane Roberts, the well-known channel for the spirit guide Seth always said, "Your point of power is in the present."

These are powerful words. You could also say "Your only power is in the present." Otherwise, there is part of your psyche that is somewhere else: hoping, remembering, and rehashing habitual thoughts that keep you from forward movement.

Action is tricky business. There is no need to push; otherwise, you are not in congruity with your deep intuitions for timing and presence. Instead, you are ahead of yourself and not in a position to find your flow. You are not taking appropriate action. You are ungrounded. If no action is taken, you are stagnating.

We fluid beings are like rivers. The watery nature of humans needs flow like water flows down a river. Too many sticks and weeds in our psyches cumulate around the rocks that are part of our riverbeds, and the river gets clogged. But you can't push the river either.

To activate the right kind of energy within you takes time and loving attention to your inner wealth of being. Restoring inner wealth is a process of years in which you gently and consistently attune to your actions and to your nature. This includes your habits: those behaviors and attitudes that feel normal and familiar and therefore are unlikely to change without some painful release. That release, and your divinity, can emerge and heal you at any moment. It is also the decision you make to enter your river and tend it well, consciously feeding, refining, revisiting, and releasing what no longer serves you.

We go through many phases in life. We can choose to evolve into better versions of ourselves and develop grace to which we didn't have access when we were younger. What gets us there is often the school of hard knocks. But we can learn from heartache and pain. We can reinterpret attitudes and hardened feelings as life experiences that made us better mothers, more considerate mates, more understanding and loving daughters.

Remember that the butterfly first goes through a gooey process that looks nothing like the caterpillar it once was nor the butterfly it will become. The startling beauty it becomes—and the experience of flight— could never be known to the creature beforehand. Yet the transformation is inevitable!

We are always in the act of becoming, so even attempting to preempt the process through control is as silly as it is impossible. Your life is a work of art so magnificent in potential that it is only in putting one foot in front of the other and trusting the process that your own butterfly essence will emerge. Like the caterpillar, who spent its life crawling about the forest floor, how can you even know what is possible for you before you actually experience the shift?

The key is to cultivate the ground of your personal transformation. You do this by incremental growth and change over time on a consistent basis. You see what is right in front of you and put all of your attention, love, energy, and thought into it.

You don't need to know the "how." Leave that to the natural unfolding of the process. Your job is only to create the vision for what you want and create a plan of action to help get you there. Your plan lives in a positive "what if" vision, where you get to play and dare and dream it up.

I am a big proponent of twenty-one day plans. Actually, it is reported that a person can completely change a habit in twenty-one days if she commits consciously and lovingly to the change. Try it soon. Choose a habit that you would like to shift, and create a doable plan for how you will focus daily to shift it.

Let's say you have been eating too many sweets. Decide that sweets will henceforth only be eaten in moderation, and allow yourself to go through a process of feeling, nibbling if need be, and noticing everything that comes to your attention over these twenty- one days. Keep saying no to having the sweets in your refrigerator and in your mind.

Keep a journal, and write about your feelings, however they emerge. Notice what you are missing—especially if you feel deprived—and any

other feelings that come up. Include thoughts on why you love sweets, how it will be so sad to be without them, and thoughts of guilt and shame that may emerge, but keep choosing to say no to actually eating them.

Start substituting other delicious food in their absence. You could buy carrot juice instead and really enjoy its sweetness. Let your intuition guide you. See what happens when you fall off your plan, but notice without judgment. If you stay with this process consciously over twenty-one days, something good may happen. You might have made a shift in your relationship with food and might draw on the strength of your resolve as you benefit more and more from your decisiveness. You might suddenly be interested in chia-seed porridge or green drinks! The practice itself will lead to the next phase.

The twenty-one day process can be used for anything you want to change in your life. I recommend "The 21-Day Consciousness Cleanse" by Debbie Ford (HarperCollins 2009) for a complete and supportive exploration of what this kind of plan can shift for you. I had many shifts of awareness while reading the book and doing all of the exercises; I encourage you to take on this project.

Any decision and dedicated action you take toward a goal, whether it is for bringing something new into your life or letting go of something that no longer serves you, will help to take back your power in the present by being strong and making a choice about what you want and what you don't want. This will serve you well as you take on more and more leadership in your business. It will make you more decisive, determined, and clear-headed about your goals. It will have impact on your relationships and your well-being in ways you can't even imagine. This process really does extend to productivity in general and creating plans for achieving your most precious goals.

Our biggest problems are stress, distraction, and disorganization. We have too many balls in the air at one time. Humans are not meant to be multi-taskers. We are meant to focus, create, develop, and complete projects and then go out for a walk! Studies have shown that we believe we are able to focus on more than one thing at a time but that we deceive ourselves and actually have less than productive results from our frenetic behavior.

Why not be kind to yourself and make healthy choices for living the way you want to live. Be strong in your conviction to plan your day in such a way that you are continually choosing to do only what is on your list of important tasks, and allow a new level of calm to come to you.

Choose to be in full awareness as you uni-task, and enjoy the simplicity and harmony that starts to enter your life. Let your nature flourish in the doing itself, and learn how to say no when confronted with something you don't want to do. Let your vision guide you on a daily and an hourly level. Get into real action with your dreams, and let your whole body drink in the glorious feeling of being awake and aware and conscious. Such a simple request, but not so doable in this era that we have so quickly entered.

Then you can start to make ninety-day plans, six-month plans, and yearly plans that you can actually accomplish in this new way. I believe ninety- day plans to be the best strategy for accomplishing goals. Once you have a simple ninety-day goal, you can arrange it into doable parts to work through all of the details in the implementation logically. You can create sub-lists and priorities that will bring the goal into fruition without procrastination, distraction, or overwhelm. Engaging in your projects with the wealth of energy-management tools at your disposal—those daily practices that we have already addressed—come to your aid in the accomplishment of the goals themselves. The process runs smoothly when you are at command central.

We can choose to be peaceful and prosperous! We can be powerful and present in our lives. It is nothing more than a decision and a choice. Choose peace within your business and simplicity. Then keep these attributes in mind while you are working.

And remember, it is good to engage and connect with your inner resources whenever possible. These are the richest and wisest aspects of yourself, which you actually have access to at any time. These aspects of your psyche are already in mastery and don't have to be improved upon. They are already within and available for consultation.

Your inner wisdom already knows the course your soul is on. You just have to figure out how to gain access to it. As you figure out how to listen to your inner guidance you will find that you don't need
advice from others to know what, when, and how you should go forward in service to your mission.

Ideally, you want to be soul-inspired at all times. You want your soul connection to be front and center in your business plans. Your wisdom enables you to gain access to the golden white light of the soul that streams down and fills every cell of your body with healing if you allow it to do so. Your soul is basically the opposite of your ego self. It is that eternal part of your being that is an aspect of Divine Presence that merges with your physical being upon birth and lives in you—as you—for your whole life then leaves when you die. It then continues in a finer, non-physical aspect until rebirth.

I know this is a radical idea, but it makes sense in terms of the continuity of your journey. It seeks out your life purpose and keeps you on course for the lessons and insights you receive in the process of exploring your work and your contribution.

I believe that the suffering you experience in life is mostly just the lack of connection or access to your soulful being. When you have lost the sense that you inherently

belong as part of the Divine spark, you begin to doubt. If you are able to maintain the soul connection at all times there is no doubt. Your very essence is soul-filled, and you can conduct your life from this anchor with assur ance that the essence of you is most magnificently expressed through your work.

I was raised in a Western tradition, and therefore my unconscious resonates with the idea of God. Eastern religions teach similar processes for becoming acquainted with the Self, but they tend to leave the concept of God out of it.

For me, our fundamental nature is God-directed. The pain and suffering we feel is the extent to which we have felt separate from God. Call it "Universal Consciousness" if the word "God" is difficult for you, but the inner work we do to connect with our essential nature is all about coming to harmony with that which is greater than us.

The soul is described through four levels of Divine connection according to Kabbalah, the Jewish Mystical Tradition that has offered spiritual direction for thousands of years. But before I describe these levels of Divine connection, I must first say that it is through our breath that we first experience our connection with the Divine. From the first story in the Bible it is stated that God "breathed into man a pure soul." We are intimately connected to God through God's desire to know us, to reveal His presence to us and through us. Our connection to God is so close that we can't even see that connection as our breath; we tend to forget to appreciate what sustains our life.

The soul journey is one of remembering this Divine source and Divine connection, and the Jewish tradition teaches us to both remember and to praise God. Imagine how your life would change if every waking moment was in praise of God? Our connection to ourselves gets stronger and more vital in this way because we are connecting ourselves to the Divine essence and agreeing that we are one and the same with it.

A way to access the insights available to this study is through the self- reflective process that we call meditation. There are many ways to meditate, and all traditions have some form of this practice. I was an early student of meditation. I came of age in the seventies after the Beatles had already gone to India to see the Hindu guru Maharishi and brought back the stories and songs of devotion and enlightenment that they had gained in his presence. Gurus were traveling to America to share their messages of inner worlds and coming with a message of the importance of connecting through oneness with God.

It seems that Western students of religion had to hear the message from the exotic East instead of within their own traditions, and I was no exception. The sixties were just a "magical mystery tour" for me, like a delicious magical kingdom suddenly opening doors to the exotic unknown. There was Buddhism, Hinduism, Taoism, Yoga, and Tai Chi: all readily available for American consumption, and consume we did!

I went to my first Ashram at the age of twenty-two and took on deep meditation journeys with thousands of other devotees. Friends were taking oaths of abstinence and moving into retreat settings to devote their lives to these practices. One of my college professors took abstinence vows and joined a Hindu Ashram. I knew of one woman who chose to go into silent retreat for twelve years! All of this made a deep impression on me. I met Amritananda Mai, the "hugging" guru, in 1990, when she was sharing her teachings with small groups on a lawn in Westchester instead of to the thousands who seek her now.

I was especially privileged to be a student of Dudjum Rimpoche, who was close friends with the Dalai Lama and a great teacher and holder of the Terton lineage of Tibetan Buddhism at a time when his teachings were accessible to only an intimate few. I remember cooking for him at his home in New York after everyone else had departed. That was one of the highlights of my life! This is called having darshan with a teacher or receiving a direct transmission of their wisdom and light.

These rich experiences had great influence on me. And, at this time, many spiritual books were coming onto the market. This was a perfect time, just before the onslaught of the information age, when we could spend hours together in the company of great teachers without feeling the need to get back to our email.

We were renaissance children, the baby boomers who had privilege and access to ideas as well as time to spend developing our spiritual lives. Generally, we did not choose to deepen the religions of our birth but, instead, travel inwardly and outwardly to the exotic and different. We were a bridge from the spiritual masters of old to a new age that brought the bounty of illumination as well as charlatry. Were we harbingers of things to come, a shift of the ages? Perhaps; at least we prepared the ground for such possibilities.

So take a moment now to think about your own spiritual life. What do you think your soul has chosen to do this time around? What mission or purpose have you been divinely ordained to pursue? Please know that your destiny path is divinely ordained. You are meant to be here; otherwise, you would have not been born. Are you a teacher, a judge, a farmer? Is it your task to bring new forms of sustenance and agriculture to the world in time to avert the catastrophes befalling us at this time? Are you a healer, a scientist? All these paths are noble. Are you a spiritual teacher and healer who is not teaching or healing others? Then you are most likely in penalty from your gifts.

The gift of meditation is unequaled in my opinion. Your ability to use this energy tool is paramount for living a life of freedom, ease, and joy. Meditation is your personal connection to the divine, which can be practiced every day and can help you develop your soul connection.

But how do you meditate? Let your definition be wide and flexible. There are all kinds of methods available for study: from simple breathing techniques (which I recommend) to much more formal and elaborate practices. The first time I meditated was in college. A friend and I decided we were going to meditate, so we sat cross-legged in a dark room and lit a candle on the floor. Then we waited to see what was going to happen. Well, something did happen for me. I followed my breath for a few minutes and then went into what one could call a mindless state of being. It was thrilling! My first experience was a deep dive into the beauty and essence of being, and all I had was a lit candle and a friend. There are no props or tools necessary to begin. You don't have to receive a secret mantra or get a special blessing from a guru. Just begin.

The difficulty with meditation is not the doing of it but in being consistent. Many teachers emphasize the quieting of the mind so that thought simply falls away; when the mind wanders, just bring it back. As Deepak Chopra was known to say, "We are human beings, not human doings." The thoughts that come interfere with our being-ness, so to cultivate the practice of meditation allows that little bit of time each day for expansion and openness instead of getting lost in past and future thinking. It is time to come fully present without an agenda. The plan is simply to be in life in all of the wholeness that you are in this moment, with no expectation and no reward.

My Tibetan practice came from Vajrayana Buddhism, which includes elaborate and accurate visualizations as well as recitation of mantra during the meditation. The commitment necessary to study in this way is well worth the trouble and will change your life, but there are other forms available that are far less time consuming.

Some practitioners devote their lives to meditation, and I am glad they are among us, but, for the Westerner, it may not be practical to spend hours a day in meditation. However, sometimes I wonder what my life would have been like had I continued on the path I started back in 1984. The woman I knew who went into silent retreat for twelve years was connected with a Buddhist Center in Woodstock, New York, and her choice to do this seemed such a crazy notion to me that I would spend hours contemplating what she must be going through. I pretended to be her in that little hut, and I imagined what she would be like after twelve years by which time her peers would had married and had children and careers.

A little less restrictive choice is to live in an Ashram for a period of time or to join a group that meditates together regularly such as the Buddhist Center to which I was connected or a center for Kabbalah. Many churches and synagogues now have programs that offer the teachings of mainstream religious observance but also honors a need of congregants for more introspective training that I am highlighting here. Even allowing twenty minutes a day for your practice will go far to bring you serenity and satisfaction because its purpose is to reveal your divinity to you. Now, what could be better than that?

My current meditation practice includes the "whispered ah" practice that I learned through studying the Alexander Technique. But any mindful awareness practice will do. These simple practices works really well for me, as there are other morning practices that I also do regularly. I start with the "whispered ah" and then allow myself to go into meditation for as long as circumstances will allow. Every once in a while, I pull out a Buddhist practice and do that as well, which is always rewarding; I'm always pleased at how fluid and easy it is to do it after so many years of dedicated practice.

Another idea is to buy a CD that has a continuous "Om" chant and sit and sing along with it. You will be surprised how peaceful you feel. Om is called the primordial sound, which is meant to resonate with our deep centers within. People have been chanting Om for thousands of years; there must be something special about it!

Meditation does bring peace into your life. It is a way to tame your impatience and emotional anxieties. It helps your body to rest while deepening the breath. It promotes the oxidation of your blood, bringing more calm to your nervous system, and it puts you in touch with your immortal being: your soul.

In Kabbalah, we speak of the four levels of the soul in order to get closer to the light of God. First, there is the physical. Called the Nefesh, it is as if the soul were being breathed into the body by God. As you breathe into this soul center within your body, feel the glorious essence of your organs and the mysterious harmony of your physical being. You can connect with, and acknowledge, that everything is working in perfect order. You can appreciate the miraculous activities always at work within to restore and replenish your life force without your needing to direct it.

I am not sure whether I heard the story through Kabbalah study, but I once was told that the angels are busy working to restore our bodies to wholeness, changing forces so that the body can continually heal at the cellular level. It is said that "for every blade of grass there is an angel hovering over it saying grow, grow." Who are we to say that angels aren't doing this restorative work on us by night? What brings life to the life force? If that stops, what happens to us?

Let yourself appreciate the intricate workings of the body and how mysteriously it heals you and sustains you. That, in itself, is a miracle! Let your breath and your mind really feel the "temple of beauty" that is you. Be grateful that you have lived to see another day and can move and speak and commune with others.

Your spirit lives in your body. Your soul will elevate your body and make it more refined and perfect. Your consciousness allows divinity to dwell within. See every cell of your body respond to this reality. Let your body do its work to keep you replenished, whole, and healthy.

The next level of soul resides in the heart, and we call this Ruach. Your heart opens you to compassion, self-care, and love for yourself and others. It is spirit dwelling within you as you. As you refine this quality, you will notice a quiet sense of purpose and harmony growing in your life. People will not disturb your equanimity, and you can be a nurturing source of empathy for those who are suffering.

You are developing your capacity to feel and to choose love. You start to live beyond duality thinking and institute a "both-and"; that is, an attitude that restores balance and often brings the resolution of difficulties instead of "right and wrong, good and bad" thinking. Your capacity to hold and resolve conflict will grow stronger.

The next level of indwelling soul is called Neshama, or the mental alignment necessary to perceive Godliness. I like to think of the story of Moses on the Mountain when the bush began to burn and God spoke to him, saying, "Where are you?" and Moses said "I am here." This story reveals the most intimate relationship between God and man. Sometimes called our higher Self, this story helps us to perceive ourselves as in the image and likeness of God.

Then there is a bridge soul energy called the Chaya, which lives as pure will and vision in the aura linking you to your soul essence. It is here where you are One with the Divine, where your essence is actually part of God, and there is no separation.

Your practice is to use your breath to move gracefully through the levels of soul so that you develop dexterity in this process of making connection with your soul and your soul with God. Allow this magnificent expansion to move you beyond the physical into the spiritual essence that you are. In this way, you anchor the knowledge that you are part of the Divine and that you most certainly belong. It is said that when you take one step toward God, God takes one hundred steps toward you.

Then the only question to ask yourself is: "How can I live more within the fulfillment of the essence of the soul?" "Who am I, and what am I supposed to do here on Earth this time around?" With these questions, you will start the process and get really clear on your purpose, so that you don't find yourself on your death-bed saying to "I know there was something I should have done!" Start asking these questions now so that you can live your true mission and purpose. Yours is a holy mission.

How do you take this out into the world? How do you create a business that reflects your life purpose? One step at a time: Take time every morning to anchor and bask in your greatness, and then allow the day to begin to flow toward the best means of expressing that greatness.

Chapter Seven: Power and Presence in Action

"Out beyond the place of wrong-doing and right-doing there is a field. I will meet you there."
-Rumi

Throughout this book, I have been suggesting that you develop platinum practices that you can do every day to support and strengthen your life. Think of these practices as spiritual muscles you are exercising so that you get more clarity and more resiliency in your intention to be fully expressed every day. The consistency is what matters. You don't want to commit to meditation one day and then forget about it for two weeks, come back to it again, and so forth. Bring your spiritual connection into your life regularly, even if you don't feel like it.

Some days will be messy, but remember that there is no judgment, so who cares anyway? It is all grist for the mill. ("Grist for the Mill" was the title of a book written by Baba Ram Dass in the middle seventies, about taking full responsibility for our lives and learning not to be too arrogant. Ram Dass was a guru for many young seekers. He and Alan Watts and Hermann Hesse pointed to a spiritual way of living that was guided by Eastern philosophy; this had a great influence on many young people who were questioning the old paradigms of the times).

As you get clear on the practices that are most helpful for you, let them grow like a candle flame, getting brighter and brighter. I have about five practices that I try to do every day, at the beginning of the day.

The first one is always to do my breathing/meditation practice, even if it is for only four or five minutes. Then, if possible, I like to get out my journal and write my intentions for the day. This could take the form of envisioning the best outcome for the day and choosing my "six rocks." This "six-rocks" concept comes from the story by Stephen

R. Covey: You put your big rocks in the jar first, so the pebbles and sand don't take the space meant for the important things: a walk in the park or exercise, or eating well but also should include a few revenue-generating activities. I believe that here is nothing you can do for your business success that is better than this practice.

After this, I do my "belief transformation" practice, which I encourage you to learn to do for yourself. You can go to my Website www.healingintoabundance.com/resources to receive the template and explanation for how to use the belief-transformation tool. We all have limiting beliefs that hold us back from living our best lives. Many of those beliefs, attitudes, and behaviors are working on the subconscious and are held in check by the ego-mind, where any risk is perceived by the ego as dangerous and therefore a crisis. This energy- transformation tool will help you shift those beliefs that you have outgrown yet are still compromising your choices and preventing you from acting on your big ideas. These outgrown beliefs are keeping you from taking the risks that will move your business— and your life— forward.

The last practice I do, if time permits, is to have a little meeting with my "divine team." Here is where you can really use your imagination and bring in anyone you want for advice: your inner business manager, your fun and play director? How about the Dalai Lama or Mother Theresa? Why not? My inner soul coach Diane knows a lot more about marketing and sales than I do, so I definitely tune in to whatever she is saying to me.

This particular practice is where I fall down the most. I simply forget that I have a divine team of loving support and guidance. Perhaps there is a part of me that still doesn't really believe that I am deserving of all that delicious guidance available just for the asking. Herein lies the difference between struggle and flow in business. Herein also lies the difference between being a follower and being a leader. This energy- management tool sets you apart from others, where you are seeking your own counsel and not looking outside yourself for approval or advice. Of course, your inner team may be saying "go out and get some expert advice." Then I suggest that you listen to that inner guidance.

Each of these platinum practices is an energy-management tool. Using even one of these tools on a regular

basis will strengthen your personal leadership potential and get you closer to acting on your dreams.

What gives you power and mastery is the practice that you do over time to increase your power and presence. As you become your own authority, you no longer look outside yourself for confirmation that you are doing exactly what is right for you to start to stand more in your power. Nobody can throw you off because you are listening to your own counsel. If things are not unfolding naturally and easily, you simply course-correct. You see clearly what is in front of you. You make decisions for yourself about the best course of action to take, and then you act on your decisions, no matter how imperfectly.

Practice is what will make you better at what you do. Do not expect that the first time you stand in front of an audience, your speech will be 100% spot-on. How could it be? Allow yourself the luxury of the learning curve and just be curious and open in the process.

Action trumps indecision. Even taking imperfect action is better than no action. I have been making a case for how very important it is for women to live and work together in community so that taking action is fun. It is getting away from your computer and moving into doing things with other people.

We are all highly conscious, creative women in this tribe, and the more we stay in the idea phase of our creations, the less action we take. This can be a trap and will prove to be your downfall if you don't develop some "chutzpah"—that is, nerve—to go after what you say you want.

We are talking about being seen. Getting out in front of an audience with a point of view and being willing to hear the response puts you in a leadership role. Remember, it is scary and dangerous to the ego-mind. There is no way that your ego would have you take such wildly adventurous actions. It is too unsafe. You will not be safe in the old way of thinking about safety. The new safe is the exhilaration of knowing that you are making your dream happen. You are out in front of other people, sharing your gifts and talents and then learning from the experience.

You are not supposed to be perfect at first. You need to just get out there and see how it goes. Inevitably, there will be someone who adores you and everything you say and someone who doesn't. Keep the adorers around as

your cheerleaders. There will also be some who challenge you from the start, and you can immediately see and sense their resistance to you; you can practice inviting them in, as you already know they will be there. They are not your people. As the saying goes, you cannot please all of the people all of the time, and those you are not pleasing are not able to learn from you how to make their lives better. As those who are not meant to work with you fall away, you are attracting the ideal clients whom you are meant to serve. It is all service anyway, so let go a little more, relax into your service offering, and know that you are doing the right things to move your dream business forward.

Your only job is to take what is in your heart and get it to the people you are meant to serve. If it lands hard for some, you must accept that they were not meant to be part of your tribe and might find the right person or people to move them forward on their evolution. If you are not getting people to raise their hands and say "yes" to you, then maybe you have to back up a few steps and get clearer on your mission and the meaning behind what you are doing.

Find out what the problem is, correct it, and you will have clients. You are not supposed to work with everybody. Most of the people you connect with will not even know that they need your services at first. It is your job to help them see that their lives will be happier and more productive with your service. If you don't feel that way now, please go back and get clear about exactly how you can help people and which urgent problem you can solve that your potential client really cares about solving. This research will support everything in your business, from what you say in your copy to how you present your signature talk, to how you have the sacred selling conversation with those who are thinking about working with you.

You must firmly believe that what you have to offer is beyond their wildest dreams about what is possible for them and you are the one to lead them to this Promised Land. It doesn't matter what the vehicle is— having a better body, losing weight or stress, building better relationships, or helping them with their marketing and sales. You might even have a product and not a service. So get behind your product one hundred percent, and find the people who need it.

You must always deliver value and quality; that goes without saying. But if you are anything like me, you probably have many letters after your name and are still thinking you are not quite ready and just need to take that one more certification or coaching program. This is where you have to get really honest with yourself, and ask if you are procrastinating on your dream because of fear. There are different kinds of procrastination, so if we can get more clear on what you are doing and how you are thinking you could refine your action plan a little bit more.

The first kind of procrastination is about clutter: is a big obstacle for some, so don't take this lightly. My chapter on de-cluttering your environment and your "in-box" and your history will go a long way to help you end this pattern of inaction. De-cluttering is an ongoing process. Papers and half-finished projects can get waylaid for months or years because of your clutter. As I mentioned earlier, getting a practical manual on Feng Shui and going through it step by step—not skipping through any of the steps—will help you put an end to this problem.

The second kind of procrastination is more emotionally driven. It takes the form of feeling like a fraud or feeling like you are not ready. This is a fear that can be overcome by going through the fear and not side-stepping it. Seeing fear as an annoying friend who is trying to "have your back" is one way of acknowledging the fear but not being taken down by it. You see this friend as an inevitable part of your life. So get on with it, and don't worry about it. It is actually the physical and psychological expression of the ego that wants—more than anything—to keep you from catastrophe.

My quick answer for this one is to spend time thinking about and acting upon things that really make you happy. Your happiness level comes, as I have said before, from a deep sense of purpose and vision. It comes from you grounding yourself in the knowledge of who you truly are in your heart of hearts and being willing to talk about those dreams and visions to others. Help them come into reality on the idea level first, so you can hear your own words and ideas being articulated. As you start to identify more with these qualities, which come directly from your desires, you are claiming your space and standing strong in your power.

Action comes out of this courage to create and to be fully expressed in your life. It shows you your destiny path. Then the opportunities that come your way can work for you instead of against you. You will say yes to them

instead of no. You can focus more on the trust and faith aspects of your business because you are not wishy-washy about what the dreams are. You are grounding them in the world, which is the first step toward manifesting. Then, if there is anxiety or fear, you are balancing the cost of not taking action with the fear and strengthening your resolve not to let inaction happen.

A third form of procrastination is not really procrastination at all; rather, it is your intuition that the time is not yet right for all of the pieces to fall into place. Timing is important, and a big part of living in flow is to acknowledge when the opportunities should and should not be acted upon. This opens you to the realm of conviction, decision, intention, and planning. And there is nothing wrong with that!

You might need to re-do your business plan, for example. You may have been operating under the auspices of an old idea of how to manage your business when a new plan for prioritizing the elements of the whole picture is right in front of you. More support and trust by hiring someone, or many people, to move your business forward might be the appropriate next step for you. This is not procrastination. Instead it draws out another mindset hurdle. It requires you to admit to yourself that you can actually handle having and paying employees. It calls on you to play a bigger game!

And why not? Do you believe you don't deserve this support? If this is so, you must strengthen your self-value. When did you decide that you did not deserve to have your dream? From whom did it come and when? Whom or what have you been serving that has taken you out of your game? A business owner must come through this process with a big "Yes, I am deserving; I am worthy."

After you have done another layer of work on these mindset setbacks, you can again focus on attracting your ideal client. Tell people that what you offer is the fulfillment of their prayers: something they have not yet allowed themselves to imagine. Your enthusiasm becomes their inspiration.

You paint the picture for them about how much better their quality of life will be after they get the gift you are offering. You express the vision for them, so that they know what the cost of not having it would be. This cost has both an emotional aspect and a financial aspect. They are probably leaving a lot of money on the table because they haven't gotten clarity on what you are offering.

Your job is to give them clarity in small, understandable portions so they can make progress toward their goals and dreams.

Goals and dreams are intricately intermingled. Some of us don't dare to dream about the possible future we could have for fear of being disappointed, but the disappointment really comes through confusion and non-action, not from the dream itself. The dream is just sitting there waiting for you to bring it into the light.

Both these issues need to be addressed in order to get into action. Confusion can be a self-sabotaging behavior. As long as one stays confused and overwhelmed, there is a built-in excuse for not having success. How can a confused person be successful? They can't. It is your job to dismantle their confusion.

Being overwhelmed is similar to confusion; it is a time-management problem and a clutter problem. This is why I am so adamant about de-cluttering and making your environment beautiful and peaceful. If you can't even find the papers you were working on the day before, how can you possibly remember all the details of the project in front of you?

Being confused and overwhelmed are often conditions that belie an underlying "conflicting intention." A conflicting intention comes from the subconscious mind that is holding two conflicting desires at the same time. You may think you want to get your soul-inspired coaching/healing practice under way but there is another subconscious desire that is stronger, which takes hold and sabotages the progress you would otherwise be making toward your goal.

It may take the form of believing that you
would not have time for your children or husband if you spent so much time doing your business and so you literally stop doing what is needed to get more visible in your niche. Or it could be coming from a deep fear of exposure, of being seen, as if you didn't feel you had the right to speak up or that you would be called out as imperfect in some way.

It is extremely important to come to terms with your conflicting intentions. Simply recognizing and admitting that you have them can go a long way to releasing the mixed-up energy and start to move you forward again.

Another reason people don't get into action is that they don't feel quite ready. This is dangerous; it harkens back to the "compare and despair" attitude. If you listen to someone else's teleclass instead of creating your own, even when you know the material inside and out, you are in danger of never getting into action. Other people will pass you by because they had the courage to go ahead and create their signature program and market it. Notice what you feel in your body when you visualize a colleague who has done that. Are you feeling envious or frustrated? This might be an indication that you have some work to do in this area.

It doesn't matter if your work is similar to a lot of other spiritual leaders or coaches. Remember that we are all in this together, so we will cross-fertilize with each other's ideas, and that is fine! Only you can put things together in exactly the way you do. And it is the resonance of your physical voice that is unique and will have positive impact on the right person. Your ideal client is waiting for you. She is already on her way to you because you have the idea and you are bringing it into a form to be received. The Universe does not operate in a vacuum. Rather, it always closes a vacuum with the creativity generated.

The creation of your products and services is the form this creativity should take. If you don't have your services clearly defined, this might be the perfect place to start. What is your super-duper BIG special VIP offering that will cost the most and to which you give the most amount of your time and devotion? What is a mid-range product or service that would not be too costly for those potential clients who want to work with you but are not ready to invest much money just yet? And what smaller program or service can you offer that will not take a good deal of your time but that will still give good value to your customers and help them solve the problems that only you can solve for them?

The beauty of this kind of a system is that there is always a next step for your client to take later. Remember, it is all about the value you offer them; therefore, there will always be a next step for them to invest in with you down the road. Your intent should be to invite them to keep saying "yes" to working with you at a higher and more invested level if that is appropriate for them. And even at your "free offering" level, you are still of service to their well-being.

This is what is commonly called your marketing funnel: big at the top and small at the bottom. Your FREE introductory product will entice your ideal client to get a taste of your services without your having to spend a great deal of time interacting with them or with the material. You could be sending a Free Report, an Assessment, or an

Audio that shares good content and provides a reason to give you their email address.

You will then have an opportunity to continue sending them tips and ideas that lead them toward an interest in receiving more high-level training or coaching/healing from you. They have entered your "tribe" and now will look forward to receiving more information through your newsletters or other low-cost offers.

Always keep in mind that it is all about the value you offer, so whatever you choose to provide must be of very high quality with significant content that they can absorb free of cost. Your motivation for doing so much gratis is to help them see the value you offer, so they will trust that you are in service to their needs and desires.

The great payoff for you is that you are no longer in hiding; you are in action. You are weaving a conscious, smart business marketing plan and offering your services at different levels for your clients. Then, depending upon how well you answer the questions that come up from those who have raised their hands to get more from you—

that is, how well you master the sacred selling conversation—you may be surprised that some of your potential clients want to go right to the top and enroll in your highest-level programs.

Some, of course, will hang around on the edges of your newsletter tribe for years until, one day, something clicks for them, and they know you are the one who is going to take them where they want to go. You are no longer "hiding, burying gifts in the sand" as one of my brilliant coaches Baeth Davis has said.

The conviction that you have something to offer that nobody else has, as well as your courage and determination to get your gifts into the spotlight, will start to pay off in more ideal clients coming your way. This will result in more sales, and you will become one with the flow of your business and your life. You will be creating a vessel in which to help potential clients land somewhere in your world, so getting really clear on your offerings should be the first step.

Imagine that you are speaking with a prospective client at a networking meeting. Imagine that when she asks you about your programs you say, "Well, I would just have you call me, and we'll do the coaching together." How do you think that person would react? She would probably think that you hadn't carefully thought through the ways you could help her. Even if you are a therapist or body/mind practitioner, you might still want to offer discounts if clients enroll in a ten-session package. By doing so, you are letting them know that your work is valuable.

F. M. Alexander, the founder of the Alexander Technique, only worked with people who would come to London and commit to a half-hour lesson five days a week for six weeks. That was his condition for anyone who would work with him. He created a parameter around his work as a pre-qualification for study with him.

Joseph Pilates is quoted as saying "With ten lessons, you will feel better; with twenty lessons, you will look better; and with thirty lessons, you will have a totally new body."

Can you hear the conviction in these two examples? My programs are now only packages of six weeks, sixteen weeks, or eight months. I am offering a choice for my clients based upon their level of interest and commitment, and I am choosing a price commensurate with the amount of time I spend with them.

You will want to give your potential clients a choice among different offerings, so the discussion is not about whether to take you up on your offer but about which one they think will best suit them, depending on their needs and concerns at the beginning of the call.

The next step is just to get the word out. How are you going to do that? You need a strategic plan. If you like to give workshops, for example, or Promo Talks, move forward on that immediately because speaking is an excellent way to promote your skills. I have given lecture/demonstrations in libraries, schools, yoga centers,

YMCAs, gyms, and even private homes. If you have three people, bring the chairs close together, and make your talk intimate. You need not worry about the number of people who show up at first. Just get the practice, and hone your skills; there is a bit of a learning curve to the art of speaking.

Whether your efforts take an online or offline form or a combination of both, the more people see your material, the better. You could write articles, blogs, or tweet little comments with links back to your site, and you are on your way in the beautiful online world.

Don't be intimidated by it, just do it. Eventually, people will notice you and start to invite you to speak. It is a natural progression, but you must choose what you are going to do strategically. Don't drop the ball when it appears that nothing is happening. Something is happening; you are becoming visibile!

Speaking engagements are important because people get a sense of you as well as your work, and the intimacy can be valuable for you. My coaching programs are focused first on all the inner work and clearing we all must do. Then, slowly grow in your confidence and poise so that you are more and more standing in your power. Your presence becomes magnetic and exciting. You become more resilient with practice, and you learn (course-correct) from your mistakes.

Nobody is perfect, and you are not expected to be perfect. You are expected to be real, so the extent to which you are willing to be vulnerable and authentic and share your story with you audience is the extent to which you will be interesting and believable to them. Being you—whether you are naturally funny, silly, even self-deprecating, if that is your nature—is what reads best to your audience: this and giving great content for them to absorb.

This might not come naturally for you. It certainly didn't come naturally for me. I had to learn by picking up on the clues of my audiences to determine whether they were with me or not. I changed over time to become more quiet and clear and honest in my teaching. I found that people responded better and learned more when I was more open and vulnerable.

Working privately, one-on-one ,was never a problem for me, but leading groups was a different matter. My stage fright emerged mightily whenever eyes were on me. And I didn't like it. I would second-guess myself and make assumptions about what audiences were thinking about me. This would cause anxiety. As soon as the spotlight off me, I would relax and breathe again. I really had to resolve this issue, or I would never have succeeded. It is interesting that I now teach people how to overcome stage fright. We always teach what we need to learn. There are processes that make it easier, many of which I have already shared with you.

What continues to surprise me, and what is revealed to me more and more, is how important it is to be vulnerable and authentic. We are not meant to be speaking from the rafters as experts, yet we grow in our expertise by speaking. It is a paradox of sorts, one that takes a lifetime to perfect. Yes some people are natural leaders and speakers. They are the workshop gurus and the talk-show celebrities, but I know from many of their disclosures that it actually takes much time, love, and self-care to develop that level of authenticity.

Women, more than men, have self-deprecating behaviors to overcome as they learn to have a voice and become visible in their business lives. Women have a long history of being told not to speak up, and sometimes those habits are frightening to break down and release. This is where levels of mindset work come in. Mindset is an energy word. Your mindset is the vibratory rate you emit. It is helpful to up-level your vibratory rate constantly, so that

you hold a higher level of prosperity and abundance in your aura and can then attract people to you instead of holding what I call a lower-level valence, where worry and self-doubt are taking hold in your consciousness.

Shifting your mindset is a lifelong process of witnessing yourself, feeling into your body, noticing when something happens that results in the "fright or flight" response (also known as startle pattern, an actual pattern of tension and contraction in your body when you have been frightened). Now we call this response "stress"; but stress can be seen and felt by others and will damage your credibility if you can't keep it in check.

My work as an Alexander Technique teacher addresses these issues of startle pattern directly and teaches a process for eliminating not the stimulus itself—because we are always going to be stimulated—but helps change response to the stimulus and make better choices about how to respond. You are actively and consciously deciding not to react to the stimulus in the habitual way, which leads to a wonderful newly found sense of freedom and control of your own life. Hooray for the Alexander Technique!

I make my Alexander work a cornerstone in helping

women prepare for the spotlight, and you will receive very specialized help from me if you enroll in either my "Step Up and SHINE!" four-month program or my more extensive eight-month VIP Diamond Elite Private Coaching Program. I would be happy to set up a time when we can explore whether this would be appropriate for you in developing a higher profile leadership role for your business. In my eight-month program, we not only do all the mindset work and the processes for becoming comfortable and charismatic while speaking to others, but we also delve into the clarity of your message, create your signature programs, and work through the offerings you are developing.

We carefully lay out both the inner-energy management elements of crafting your business; clearing the limiting thoughts, beliefs, and behaviors that have been stopping you in your tracks; and create a strategic plan to move your business forward naturally, so that you love what you are doing and get paid handsomely for it.

Your talents and your mission should go hand in hand. My intention for you is that you bound out of bed each morning, ready to do more in the creation of your soul-

inspired business. I want you to have all the pieces in place to know precisely what to do and when to do it so that you never fall backward, second-guess, or doubt yourself.

You build your business on the pillars of your soul's purpose, not on someone else's idea of what you can accomplish. You are building your dream one magical step at a time, and you are never left alone wondering what comes next. Remember that course-correcting is your best ally, and you are doing your daily platinum practices to increase your vibration and wealth consciousness as well as your poise, power, and presence. You are on fire because you have developed your confidence with elegance and ease.

Are you ready?

About the Author

Diane Young Sussman, is the second child among four "Air Force brats." Her early memories were of traversing the country in an old Oldsmobile station wagon, moving often and also visiting relatives in Minnesota every summer. Later settling in Michigan, Diane finished college, with a B.A. in Social Psychology and later a Certification in the Alexander Technique. While living in a cottage on Lake Michigan she developed a deep trust in the beauty of the Earth, and then ventured to New York to learn from the modern dance giants Erick Hawkins and Martha Graham.

Her studies also led her to the New Age leaders Joseph Campbell, Jean Houston, and the Living Theater. Always involved with collectives, Diane co-created "Theater of the Heart," a not-for-profit dance company. In her own creative movement work, called "Doorways to the Self," she led her students through movement and mind/body explorations. She later shared other movement/sound/poetry ventures with a group inspired by Rick Jarow, called

"Temple of Beauty." Diane choreographed and performed in more than twenty concerts from 1983 to 2000.

In 1987, Diane graduated from the American Center for the Alexander Technique and began her private teaching practice, helping people change their relationship to the body and mind by using the very elegant and powerful tools that Alexander work brings. She expanded her reach when she was invited to teach at the school, where she stayed for more than 23 years. During that period, Diane also became certified in Cranio-Sacral Therapy. For more than six years, she apprenticed with healer Ron Young in his Healing Wisdom School.

In 2009 Diane trained as a Spiritual LifeCoach and has been working with women to develop their innate soul connection and lead lives of power and presence in whichever field they are most drawn.

Diane has always had a great love of music and dance and has exuberance for life and learning that has kept her in a seeking—and now a leadership—role for her clients and students. She weaves in the creativity and passion she has always been drawn toward in her unique coaching style, leaving no stone unturned for the generous support she offers in service to others. Diane believes that living a life of creative self-expression is the best way to bring meaning into one's life, and she shows up ready to bring her freedom-based lifestyle forward for others to model and enjoy.

A personal note to you:

I invite you to consider jumping in and becoming one of my private clients so that you can receive the full measure of my coaching programs. (You would know intuitively if this is right for you). We go into the energy-management tools in a deep and reassuring way in order to uncover your true power and presence: your unique beauty and essence. We clear the obstacles that are still standing in your way, renew your mind and heart, and up-level your professional brand. You get to practice the energy tools that will help you clear money beliefs held on from childhood and do the inner mindset work to help you to hold a strong sense of self while delivering your beautiful work in the world. Email me at Diane@healingintoabundance.com and we can set up a time to talk. This is the most valuable work that you can ever do for yourself. It will have long-lasting benefits for your life and in your business.

Then we progress to to healing and the visioning of your future Self, starting from where you are now, and then creating a doable action plan for your next steps in creating yourmanifestations, based on the desires of your heart and the work you love. The beauty of this kind of coaching is that it works with both the emotional alignment practices (inner work) AND the outer strategies and processes that are necesary to grow your soul-inspired business. You could come for a two day VIP experience, or over a three or six month container for shifting your limiting beliefs; that is anything standing in your way from being the beautiful light that you are meant to be. Then, you may find that you are swiftly gaining the impact and income that you desire and deserve.

‎roduct-compliance